I08833358

Public Planet Books

A series edited by Dilip Gaonkar, Jane Kramer,
Benjamin Lee, and Michael Warner

Public Planet Books is a series designed by writers in and outside the academy—writers working on what could be called
narratives of public culture—to explore questions that ur-
gently concern us all. It is an attempt to open the scholarly
discourse on contemporary public culture, both local and
international, and to illuminate that discourse with the kinds
of narrative that will challenge sophisticated readers, make
them think, and especially make them question. It is, most
importantly, an experiment in strategies of discourse, combining reportage and critical reflection on unfolding issues
and events—one, we hope, that will provide a running narrative of our societies at this particular fin de siècle. Public
Planet Books is part of the Public Works publication project
of the Center for Transcultural Studies, which also includes
the journal *Public Culture* and the Public Worlds book series.

Powerless by Design

public planet books

Powerless by
Design

The Age of the International Community

Michel Feher

DUKE UNIVERSITY PRESS   *Durham and London 2000*

© 2000 Duke University Press

All rights reserved

Printed in the United States of

America on acid-free paper ∞

Typeset by Tseng Information

Systems, Inc. in Bodoni Book

Library of Congress Cataloging-

in-Publication Data appear on

the last printed page of this book.

For Amanda and Laszlo

Contents

Preface

Sometime in the early 1990s, Western officials began portraying themselves as the leading members of the international community. In that capacity, they devised a doctrine that was not only at odds with the rhetoric of the cold war but also a far cry from the "new world order" promoted by George Bush and Margaret Thatcher at the outset of the decade. Whereas their predecessors had invested almost every regional conflict with a political and ideological stake—whether it was the struggle between the "Free World" and totalitarianism or the defense of international law against rogue states—the representatives of the new international community claimed that the crises they were confronted with called neither for military intervention nor even partisan involvement on their part. Exemplary of this new approach was the Western response to the ethnic cleansing campaigns in the former Yugoslavia and the genocide of the Rwandan Tutsis. Arguing that these crimes needed to be traced to ancient tribal enmities, rather than the ideology of the regimes that had planned them, U.S. and European leaders professed that the role of the international community should be limited to a humanitarian, impartial, and conciliatory engagement with all the warring parties. Hence the tone of powerless righteousness—or was it righteous powerlessness?—that characterized Western diplomacy between the end of the Gulf War and the launching of the air campaign against Serbia in March 1999.

Faced with this new doctrine, both the liberal and radical wings of the Western Left found themselves in an uneasy position. Liberals, while lured by the vocabulary of their leaders—the latter's mottoes were indeed dialogue, the rule of law, and reconciliation—could not help feeling disturbed by the dismal results of the policies carried out in the name of the international community. Conversely, anti-imperialist militants were quick to mock the hypocrisy of their governments' helpless indignation, yet certainly not prepared to demand that Western powers resort to more forceful measures, whether in the Balkans or central Africa. Thus, if the representatives of the international community were rarely praised for their reactions to ethnic cleansing and genocide, even the traditionally critical segments of their public opinions did not present them with a particularly vigorous challenge.

With the intervention of the North Atlantic Treaty Organization (NATO) in Kosovo, however, Western leaders unexpectedly departed from what was now their time-honored doctrine. To justify their decision to confront Slobodan Milosevic without a mandate from the United Nations Security Council, the sponsors of operation "Allied Force" declared that they were acting not as the representatives of the international community but as the guardians of democracies' duty to prevent massive human rights violations. Among other consequences—especially for the Albanian Kosovars and later the people of East Timor—this sudden doctrinal shift enabled both liberal and radical activists to finally find their post–cold war marks: the former welcomed the newfound resolve of their governments as the belated fulfillment of the promises raised by the end of the cold war, while the latter condemned it as the return of the imperialist new world order. A year later, the war against Serbia continued to be a defining issue for the Western Left. Anti-imperialist militants were still working on a revisionist account of the Kosovo crisis that would vindicate their opposition to NATO's intervention, whereas liberals desperately hung onto the notion that their governments were now committed to oppose massive human rights violations, even at the expense of state sovereignty. Yet, at the same time, U.S. and European responses to the destruction of Chechnya by Russian troops seemed to indicate that the spring of 1999 had been less a turning point than an exceptional moment in the ongoing age of the international community. Therefore, while the following pages are almost exclusively about the 1990s, the discursive strategy that they attempt to expose may well remain with us for quite some time.

This book not only owes its existence to the generous encouragements and insightful critiques of some wonderful people but also to their insightful encouragements and generous critiques. I wish to express my deepest gratitude to Amanda Bay, Judith Butler, Andrea Dooley, Eric Fassin, Hal Foster, Carla Hesse, Thomas Keenan, Thomas Laqueur, Ramona Naddaff, Robert Post, Peter Sahlins, and Michael Warner. If, as I fear, my efforts have not met what their intelligence and kindness deserve, it only shows that I am a better judge of character than they are. I also want to thank my successive editors at Duke University Press: Richard Morrison, Leigh Anne Couch, and Ken Wissoker. Finally, I am very grateful to Laszlo Feher for losing hardly any sleep over this project.

Powerless by Design ━━━━━

A Puzzling Chiasma

n June 10, 1999, as Serbian troops were starting to leave Kosovo, Bill Clinton justified NATO's operation Allied Force in the following way. "We should remember," the president said in his address to the nation, "that the violence we responded to in Kosovo was the culmination of a ten-year campaign by Slobodan Milosevic, the leader of Serbia, to exploit ethnic and religious differences in order to impose his will on the lands of the former Yugoslavia. That's what he tried to do in Croatia and in Bosnia, and now in Kosovo." Throughout the century, Clinton added, "millions of innocent people died . . . because democracies reacted too late to evil and aggression." Thanks to NATO's resolve, however, this unfortunate tendency to "appease" bloody dictators by turning a blind eye to the plight of their victims was finally interrupted. The president of the United States could thus proudly conclude that "the twentieth century is ending not with helpless indignation but with a hopeful affirmation of human dignity and human rights for the twenty-first century."

This was not the first time that Clinton blamed the war in the former Yugoslavia on the "renegade regime of Slobodan Milosevic." He had already used that same expression in July 1992 as the Democratic candidate for the presidential election.[1] Soon after, on August 3, 1992, when *Newsday* correspondent Roy Gutman revealed the existence of concentration camps set up by the Serbs in northwestern Bosnia, the former governor of Arkansas was among the few Western politicians who called for an immediate military intervention. More important, the future president already defended his position as he would seven years later, namely, by stressing the necessity of confronting "ethnicist" regimes early on in order to prevent them from realizing their genocidal projects. "If the horror of the Holocaust taught us anything," Clinton declared, "it is the high cost of remaining silent and paralyzed in the face of genocide." Roger Cohen reports that just one day later, the Democratic candidate confirmed his statement by saying, "We cannot afford to ignore what appears to be a deliberate and systematic extermination of human beings based on their ethnic origin. I would begin with air power against the Serbs, to try to restore the basic conditions of humanity."[2]

Yet, starting in early 1993, the Clinton administration portrayed the Bosnian conflict in quite a different manner. Almost as soon as they took office, the new president and his secretary of state, Warren Christopher, ceased to point to the "renegade regime of Slobodan Milosevic" as the root cause of the war. Instead, they resorted to the "ancient enmity" explanation that the Bush administration had used to justify its neutrality and that was still the official line of the secretary general of the United Nations (UN) as well as the French and British governments. According to that view, what had successively set Croatia and Bosnia aflame was not the implementation of a specific political project—that is, the constitution of an ethnically cleansed Greater Serbia—but the resurgence of a traditional cultural feature of the Balkans—namely, age-old "ethnic violence" between Serbs, Croats, and Bosnian Muslims. Drawing from this "historical" perspective, George Bush's secretary of state, Lawrence Eagleburger, had famously concluded that "until the Bosnians, Serbs, and Croats decide to stop killing each other, there is nothing the outside world can do about it."[3]

Similarly, in the spring of 1993, Clinton declared that "the hatred between all three groups is almost unbelievable. It's almost terrifying, and it's centuries old. That really is a problem from hell."[4] Though some mild efforts were made to decrease the discrepancy between the positions of candidate and President Clinton — such as conceding that "the Serbs" were responsible for more atrocities than the other "warring factions," while Muslim civilians were the principal victims of the conflict — for two and a half years, the Clinton administration maintained that an extraordinarily long history of mutual resentment was the main obstacle to establishing peace in Bosnia. "Their enmities go back five hundred years, some would say almost a thousand years," said Clinton in June 1995, just a few weeks before Bosnian Serb General Ratko Mladic and his henchmen were to commit the worst genocidal act of the Bosnian War — the mass execution of over 7,000 people in the eastern enclave of Srebrenica.[5]

Even after the Dayton Peace Agreement was signed, in November 1995, the Clinton administration continued to attribute the difficulties in consolidating peace and fostering reconciliation between the three Bosnian communities to the intractability of their ancient hatreds. Similarly, in 1998, when an increasing number of Albanian Kosovars realized that they could not hope to shake the apartheid rule imposed on them by Milosevic without resorting to armed struggle, U.S. officials not only stuck to their usual "evenhandedness," apportioning blame equally between Albanian "terrorism" and Serbian "brutal repression"; true to form, they also traced these regrettable outbursts of violence to ancient enmity, this time between Serbs and Albanian Kosovars.[6] Yet once Milosevic bluntly refused to sign the Rambouillet agreements, in the winter of 1999, thereby forcing the United States and its European allies either to take military action or fatally compromise NATO's credibility, the ancient enmity explanation was suddenly dropped. In its stead, the Clinton administration revived the diagnosis of the Yugoslav wars that had been proffered by candidate Clinton in the summer of 1992. Within a few days of March 24, 1999—that is, as soon as it became clear that Milosevic would try to outlast NATO's resolve—the violence that had successively engulfed Croatia, Bosnia, and now Kosovo was no longer linked to 500 or even 1,000 years of ethnic hatred but to a decade-old renegade regime whose representatives had relentlessly endeavored to rid what they saw as Serbian land of its non-Serbian population.

Though he proved remarkably swift in substituting Milosevic's ten-year campaign for the thousand-year enmity rationale, Clinton was hardly the only one to modify his perspective on the Yugoslav wars once NATO planes started bombing Serbia. Just as striking as the president's was the symmetrical but opposite shift that took place in some leftist circles. For reasons that will be discussed at the end of this book, it is true that neither ethnic cleansing in the former Yugoslavia nor even genocide in Rwanda ever became prominent motives of outrage among what used to be called the anti-imperialist Left—in the United States as well as Europe.[7] Nonetheless, a venerable platform for U.S. progressives such as the *Nation* took a largely negative view of the West's response to the Bosnian War.

The "peacekeeping" mission known as the United Nations Protection Force (UNPROFOR), which embodied the humanitarian and impartial approach chosen by Western governments, came under especially harsh criticism in the leftist weekly in the wake of Srebrenica's fall. Columnist Christopher Hitchens, who was then representative of the *Nation*'s position, rejected the claim made by UN and Western officials that they had been "powerless" to prevent Mladic's troops from seizing Srebrenica—officially a "safe haven" under UNPROFOR protection—and slaughtering the town's male population. According to Hitchens, the fact that U.S. and European diplomats even dared to make that assertion only exposed the hypocrisy of their alleged commitments to the defense of human rights and advancement of international justice. Because the territorial integrity of a multiethnic Bosnia presented no economic or strategic interest for the United States and its allies, Hitchens argued that Western powers were simply seeking to present the partition of the country, and thus the victory of the ethnic cleansers, as a regrettable fait accompli: "The decision to let Srebrenica 'go' was a cold one," he wrote, "designed to shrink the territory claimed by the Sarajevo government and thus to create 'on the ground' the preconditions for partition. It is therefore not true to say that the shame of the West lies in watching helplessly as a population was put to the sword. The shame lies in the complicity and the collusion."[8]

5

In spring 1999, the *Nation* was still intent on exposing the hypocrisy of U.S. and European leaders. This time, however, Western governments were not faulted for claiming to be powerless in the face of systematic mass murder and deportation but for pretending that the purpose of NATO's intervention in Kosovo was to oppose such crimes. With the exceptions of UN correspondent Ian Williams and Hitchens—whose column now truly deserved to be called "Minority Report"— the *Nation*'s editors and contributors made it their mission to reject the notion that the air campaign against Serbia was an "ethical war," as British Prime Minister Tony Blair had called it, waged for humanitarian motives.[9] In about twenty editorials and articles devoted to the operation, they argued that Allied Force was not about protecting the Albanian Kosovars since the main cause of their suffering was "the blood-lust roused by NATO's bombing."[10] Rather, it was primarily about finding a new raison d'être for the North Atlantic alliance, undermining the authority of the UN, and allowing the Pentagon to show that it could wage a war without U.S. casualties.[11]

In 1995, the *Nation* had pointed to the lack of Western interests in the former Yugoslavia to explain why NATO planes did not prevent Milosevic's subcontractors from entering Srebrenica; in 1999, however, the same publication pointed to the imperialistic aims of the West to explain why NATO members used air power to pressure Milosevic into removing his troops from Kosovo. In the summer of 1995, the *Nation* had accused Western governments of hiding behind a deliberately counterproductive UN diplomacy in order to evade their own responsibilities in the victory of the ethnic cleansers; conversely, in the spring of 1999, *Nation* editorials proclaimed that Western leaders were waging a blatantly illegal war because NATO's air campaign against Serbia had been launched without the approval of the UN Security Council. In short, Western leaders, who had been blamed in 1995 for doing what they finally ceased to do four years later, were criticized in 1999 for not reverting back to their earlier policies.[12]

A remarkable feature of these two sudden and symmetrical shifts in perspective is that neither the Clinton administration nor the *Nation* felt the need to acknowledge them. Usually, for the sake of preserving some credibility among their target audiences—who as voters or readers, exercise some influence over their fate—both the U.S. government and an established voice of leftist opposition are expected to submit what they say about any particular issue to a basic set of constraints. At the very least, the stories they tell must pay homage to the values that they are supposed to stand for, convey a measure of continuity with their previous statements about the same or even related issues, and address the facts that other sources of information have made available to the public. Though public stances are subject to occasional revisions, these changes in outlook tend to be publicly acknowledged and properly framed, if only to ward off embarrassing questions. Thus, the appearance of a new rationale can either be justified by a transformation in the situation itself—such as when Ronald Reagan officially declared that Mikhail Gorbachev's Soviet Union no longer was the "evil empire"—or staged as carefully calibrated apologies—such as when Clinton recognized that the international community, including the United States, had failed to stop the Rwandan genocide.

Yet, in the spring of 1999, neither the representatives of the U.S. government nor the editors of the *Nation* tried to explain why they were modifying their views on the Yugoslav wars, whether by calling forth the good reasons or confessing the bad ones behind the incompatibility between their successive positions. The Clinton administration, far from dramatizing the replacement of the thousand-year-old-enmity explanation with the newfound indictment of Milosevic's ten-year-old renegade regime, endeavored to stress the constancy of U.S. policies. On the one hand, to prevent their current resolve from underscoring their past inaction, government officials argued that operation Allied Force belonged to the same forceful approach, albeit on a larger scale, as operation "Deliberate Force"—the bombing of Bosnian Serb positions, in the late summer of 1995, that paved the way for the Dayton Peace Agreement. But on the other hand, to avert domestic as well as international fears of a militaristic turn in U.S. foreign policy, the Clinton administration kept calling the 1999 air campaign a "humanitarian intervention," thereby suggesting some continuity between the decision to remove Serbian troops from Kosovo by force and that of sending "humanitarian aid" to Bosnia—prior to 1995—instead of military assistance.

As for the *Nation,* opposing the war against Serbia enabled the leftist weekly to return to the anti-imperialist rhetoric devised for the Gulf War: conflicts should be resolved through negotiations rather than war; public money should be spent to help people live better rather than to kill them; Western powers, especially the United States, do not have the moral right, given their own record, to impose their will on others. However, little effort was made to reconcile this familiar mix of pacifism and disgust for Western arrogance with the critique of Western hypocrisy and indifference to the victims of post–cold war conflicts that had increasingly informed the *Nation*'s view of Western diplomacy during the period ranging from the end of operation "Desert Storm" to the launching of Allied Force.

The fact that the Clinton administration obscured its own decision to publicly blame the bloody decomposition of the former Yugoslavia on a political project rather than a cultural trait suggests that this decision was not premeditated. Indeed, we have already mentioned that at the outset of the crisis leading to operation Allied Force, U.S. officials still framed the troubles in Kosovo as the resurgence of an old and intractable dispute fueled by extremists on both sides. On February 23, 1998, for instance, Assistant Secretary of State Robert Gelbard denounced the then-surging Kosovo Liberation Army (KLA) as a "terrorist group," thereby equating the proponents of Albanian armed resistance with overt advocates of Albanian deportation such as Vojislav Seselj and his Serbian Radical Party. To counter these "extremist" forces as well as to devise a compromise combining Serbian sovereignty over Kosovo and the end of the apartheid rule in there, Washington called on "moderates" such as Ibrahim Rugova, the pacifist president of the Democratic League of Kosovo, but also the supposedly "pragmatic" head of the Yugoslav state, Milosevic himself.[13]

Though the persistent defiance of the Serbian leader gradually made such evenhandedness untenable, until the end of March 1999, the U.S. government and its European allies continued to believe that Milosevic would not want to sacrifice his status as a tough-yet-indispensable partner for peace—a status that the Clinton administration had granted him during the Bosnian peace negotiations in 1995.[14] While U.S. officials realized that the Yugoslav president would test their resolve, and thus that they should be prepared to actually resort to force, they nonetheless envisioned this eventuality as a new version of operation Deliberate Force, the three-week air campaign against Mladic's forces that purported to lower the territorial ambitions of the Bosnian Serbs but also enabled Milosevic to negotiate in their name. In other words, before it was launched, operation Allied Force was not meant to be a response to a ten-year reign of terror: its initial purpose consisted of leveling the field between the Albanian and Serbian parties in order to pressure the latter into removing its troops, reinstating Kosovo's autonomy, and allowing NATO troops to monitor the peace. Among Western diplomats, the consensus was that Milosevic planned to use the threat of a NATO air campaign, or even endure a few days of largely symbolic bombing, to persuade the Serbian people that for the sake of their safety, he had no other choice than to comply with the terms of the Rambouillet agreement that he had previously refused to sign. Accordingly, not only did NATO governments fail to prepare for a protracted war but they went as far as announcing publicly that they had no intention of deploying ground troops in Kosovo prior to the departure of the Serbian special forces.

Once the bombing of Serbia began, however, U.S. and European officials realized that they had considerably overestimated Milosevic's fear of becoming an international pariah. (They may have thought that he would not want to expose his country to the lot of Iraq after the Gulf War, whereas the main lesson Milosevic had drawn from Desert Storm was that, nine years later, Saddam Hussein was still in power.) Betting both on the fragility of NATO's unity and Russian support for the Serbian cause, the Yugoslav leader challenged Western governments to sustain a long campaign. Moreover, taking advantage of their refusal to commit ground troops, he ordered his army to empty Kosovo of its Albanian population—thereby fulfilling the covert promise on which he had built his power in the late 1980s. Thus, it was only when the Clinton administration understood that the war, though still undeclared, was going to last longer, kill more civilians—the infamous "collateral damages"—and raise more anti-American sentiments than initially expected, that its representatives sought to secure the support of the U.S. public by providing a new definition of the violence that successively ravaged a third of Croatia, the whole of Bosnia, and now Kosovo.

Portraying the difference between the various Yugoslav "warring parties" in purely quantitative terms—that is, one of them had more weapons at its disposal and was guilty of more crimes than its rivals—had proved a good enough formula as long as U.S. officials merely needed to justify the threat or even limited use of force as a proper way to pressure the dominant and more brutal party into negotiating with its weaker foes. But when NATO was suddenly faced with the prospect of a prolonged and hazardous confrontation with Serbia, the Clinton administration could no longer defend its involvement without proclaiming that the difference between Milosevic and his enemies, past and present, was a qualitative one—namely, the Serbian leader had relentlessly endeavored to "exploit ethnic and religious differences in order to impose his will on the lands of the former Yugoslavia."

While Milosevic's unexpected gamble pressured Clinton and his aides into hastily modifying their official diagnosis of the Yugoslav conflicts, in turn, the new rationale adopted by U.S. and NATO officials compelled the editors of the *Nation*—and more generally, the exponents of the anti-imperialist Left—to hurriedly reframe their own critique of Western policies in the former Yugoslavia. Given the record of U.S. and European governments throughout the 1990s, in the Balkans as well as central Africa, leftist activists were understandably unprepared for Clinton and Blair's defense of an ethical war waged in the name of human rights. Forced to improvise a quick response, they railed against Allied Force with a collection of makeshift and mostly weak arguments. As already mentioned, the latter included traditional pacifist outcries—such as California state senator Tom Hayden asserting that the war against Serbia was fought at the expense of "school lunches and seniors' prescriptions"—and righteous denunciations of the true motives behind NATO's intervention in Kosovo.[15]

Other arguments designed to rally the leftist opposition to NATO's war were not only weak but strangely flawed. For instance, several articles in the *Nation* and elsewhere, while correctly underscoring the contradiction between the humanitarian end claimed by the sponsors of operation Allied Force and the means they used to achieve it—that is, an air campaign that left Serbian ethnic cleansers undeterred—nonetheless concluded that deploying ground troops in Kosovo would be an even greater "folly" than bombing Serbia from the sky. Another example, albeit one with a long history, consisted of faulting Western powers for showing a selective moral sense. Why should we approve of NATO's intervention on behalf of the Kosovars, the reasoning went, when the same Western leaders who vow not to let Milosevic's atrocities go unpunished all but condone the dirty war of the Turkish government against the Kurds, the continued occupation of Palestinian land by Israel, and China's brutal subjection of Tibet?[16]

Hardly more persuasive, but revealing of how the ethical war rationale had taken the anti-imperialist Left by surprise, was the contention that the U.S. government, possibly with the help of its British ally, had deliberately sabotaged the Rambouillet negotiations. Popular among contributors to the *Nation, Le Monde diplomatique,* and *Il Manifesto,* but also with Russian and Chinese officials, this argument was based on two facts: first, Secretary of State Madeleine Albright—unquestionably the most ardent foe of Milosevic within the Clinton administration—had persuaded the Albanian delegation to sign the Rambouillet agreement by promising them a referendum on the final status of Kosovo after three years; and second, the Pentagon demanded that the final document include a so-called "annex b," according to which NATO troops would not only have the right to patrol Kosovo but also to bivouac and even arrest individuals in the entire territory of the Federal Republic of Yugoslavia. Because Albright's pledge paved the way for Kosovo's independence while the Pentagon's request impinged on Serbia's sovereignty, leftist critics maintained that the intention behind these two clauses was to make the whole accord unacceptable for the Serbian party, thereby giving NATO a pretext to intervene.

Why, after sparing Milosevic for so many years, would the Clinton administration be suddenly so keen on launching a military operation against him? And if a pretext to punish Serbia was what the president and his aides were after, why didn't they plan a ground invasion—at least for the sake of intimidating Milosevic—and why did they proclaim to have no intention of deploying infantry troops prior to the departure of Serbian forces? The advocates of the "U.S. warmongering" argument never answered these questions. But even the two facts they cited to show that the Clinton administration was actually looking for war fail to support their contention.

The demands made by the U.S. military at Rambouillet, though clearly offensive to Milosevic, certainly did not betray a desire on the part of the Pentagon to have its soldiers either invading Serbia or even roaming through Yugoslav territory; quite the contrary. Coming from arguably the most isolationist institution in the United States, "annex b" merely expressed the military's obsessive concern for the security of its own troops.[17] As for Secretary Albright's last-minute promise to the Albanian delegation, far from conveying some secret and bellicose agenda, it once again pointed to the improvised character of Western diplomacy in Kosovo. Fashioned after the Dayton Peace Agreement, the initial version of the Rambouillet agreement comprised three major tenets: restoring Kosovo's pre-1989 status, namely, that of an autonomous province of Serbia; mandating NATO troops to keep the peace and monitor the implementation of the agreement; and pressuring both sides into signing the agreement by, respectively, threatening the Serbs with military intervention and warning the Albanians that if they rejected the plan, they would be left alone with Milosevic. What this framework failed to consider, however, was that after ten years of apartheid and one year of systematic ethnic cleansing, the Kosovars, whether "moderates" or "extremists," could not agree to less than the prospect of independence, even if it meant fighting for it without Western support. Thus, as the Rambouillet conference was heading for disaster, Western officials realized that unless they gave some hope to the Albanian side that Kosovo would not always remain under Serbian sovereignty, they themselves would soon have to choose between letting yet another genocide take place without reacting and planning for massive military intervention.[18]

Whether weak, flawed, or disingenuous, all the ill-constructed arguments through which the anti-imperialist Left intended to mobilize its supporters against NATO's intervention in Kosovo showed that progressive voices such as the *Nation* did not expect to be confronted with the ethical war rationale devised to justify Allied Force. But what was maybe even more embarrassing than opposing NATO's new mandate with bad arguments was the fact that by virtue of these arguments, leftist critics of Western governments were simply adopting the latter's previous position vis-à-vis the Yugoslav conflicts. Indeed, the *Nation*'s idea of a suitable alternative to NATO's air campaign was a new round of negotiations, minus the threat of force, with Milosevic in order to broker an arrangement acceptable to the Serbian party. Such an agreement would have involved Milosevic's promise to let some Albanian refugees—presumably those who could prove they were not related to "terrorists"—return to their destroyed villages, while an unarmed UN contingent ("with Russia and non-NATO forces in a central role") kept the peace.[19] In other words, what the *Nation* advocated was a caricature of the disastrous UNPROFOR mission in Bosnia that had been vigorously denounced, at the time, in the pages of the leftist weekly. Hence the reluctance, among the *Nation* editors, to reckon with their own shift in perspective.[20]

The purpose of stressing the contradictions in the successive positions taken by the Clinton administration and by its leftist critics is not to dismiss the words spoken by the president or printed in the *Nation* as the disposable instruments of their respective interests. Obviously, U.S. officials always need to proclaim that the policies of their government are principled, while *Nation* readers expect their favorite weekly to explain why they are not. So long as Clinton was determined to avoid a military intervention in Bosnia, his representation of the Yugoslav wars as the resurgence of a thousand-year-old ethnic enmity supported his claim that the United States was power-less to stop the bloodshed, while giving the *Nation* the oppor-tunity to expose this alleged powerlessness as thinly veiled indifference and neglect. Conversely, as soon as Clinton de-cided to force Milosevic's troops out of Kosovo by launching an air campaign against Serbia, his sudden reframing of the conflict as the work of a ten-year-old renegade regime helped to vindicate his decision, while giving the *Nation* the opportu-nity to brand operation Allied Force as a display of unrecon-structed Western imperialism. Yet, the fact that the Clinton administration and the *Nation* happened to hold two consecu-tive positions that were both mutually exclusive and perfectly self-serving should not be interpreted as an argument against examining their public stances in their own right. For no mat-ter how cynical and self-interested we imagine either of them to be, even if we believe that the Clinton administration was primarily concerned with putting a high-minded face on its hegemonic designs while the *Nation*'s main preoccupation consisted of maintaining an impeccably anti-Western record, we still have to recognize that the stakes in both cases were modified by the rationales through which they pursued their respective agendas.

Simply by virtue of claiming that democracies have a duty to prevent "evil and aggression," and that putting an end to Milosevic's ten-year campaign of systematic ethnic cleans-ing was part of that obligation, Clinton undeniably defined a new framework for the narratives concerning U.S. foreign policy—regardless of whether we believe in the sincerity of his claim. Because the Serbian leader is hardly the only head of a post–cold war state who sought to secure his rule by fueling ethnic hatred, a doctrine according to which "democ-racies" should be expected to rescue any group that is per-secuted on the basis of its race, ethnic origin, or religious faith is destined to both offer new opportunities and raise new problems for the country that Secretary of State Albright has called the "indispensable nation."

As far as opportunities are concerned, any U.S. adminis-tration may have an easier time organizing an international operation against a regime inimical to U.S. interests if it ad-heres to a doctrine whereby any state oppressing one of its own national minorities triggers democracies' commitment to "human dignity and human rights," and thus faces a mili-tary intervention led by the United States. Indeed, consid-ering the nature of the regimes that have challenged U.S. hegemony since the end of the cold war—from Hussein to Milosevic's—it is safe to assume that in the near future, the most likely threats to the "vital" interests of the United States will continue to come from nationalist governments with a particularly poor human rights record.

As far as the problems that Clinton's defense of Allied Force might cause for U.S. foreign policy, they stem from the same alleged duty to forcefully respond to systematic perse-cution. While such an obligation might facilitate the stigma-tization of governments inimical to U.S. interests, insofar as it were rigorously interpreted, there is little doubt that it would prove more burdensome than beneficial. First, as the lead-ing power among democratic nations, the U.S. government might find it difficult to avoid getting involved in conflicts that were previously kept at arm's length on the grounds that they were the unfortunate result of intractable ethnic hatreds. Second, and even more serious, U.S. diplomats might have a considerably harder time justifying their administration's support of longstanding allies whose treatment of minori-ties verges on evil and aggression. Furthermore, considering China and Russia's steadfast attachment to the inviolability of national sovereignty—amply demonstrated by the former's policies in Tibet and the latter's record in Chechnya—if the United States and its British ally actually intended to generalize the "ethical" justification they gave to NATO's intervention in Kosovo, they could do it only at the cost of returning the UN Security Council to its state of cold war paralysis. Fourth, given the Pentagon's reluctance to expose U.S. soldiers—and even expensive material—unless it is in what the military see as the vital interests of the United States, an administration intending to make good on Clinton's commitment to human dignity and human rights is bound to have a troubled relationship with its own armed forces. Finally, even if Washington continues to deny the competence of the future International Criminal Court, the fact that independent prosecutors and judges have recently been able to indict former or even sitting heads of state for crimes against humanity might make it increasingly difficult for U.S. officials to pick and choose the targets of democracies' righteous outrage.

Painfully aware of these problematic prospects, some prominent members of the Clinton administration were quick to lower the standards set by the president's "victory" speech. National Security adviser Sandy Berger, for example, argued that while the U.S. government condemned atrocities wherever they were committed, it was nonetheless the particular purpose and capacities of NATO that had made operation Allied Force possible. In other words, Berger conveyed that Europe was the only region where democracies following the lead of the United States were in a position to prevent evil and aggression—especially in the absence of an explicit UN mandate. As for Clinton himself, he refused to restrict the new commitment he had just assigned to democracies to European soil. To the contrary, in his already mentioned address to the nation he emphatically declared it applicable "to the people of the world, whether you live in Africa or in Central Europe or any other place." In the same breath, however, the president made sure to qualify his promise by saying that the democracies in the name of which he was speaking would stop racial, ethnic, or religious persecution if "it is within our power to stop it."

That this latter qualification could prove as restrictive as the one offered by Berger was already apparent in the initial reaction — or absence thereof — of the administration to the massacres and massive deportation perpetrated by the Indonesian army and paramilitary in East Timor, barely three months after NATO troops entered Kosovo. Yet, no matter how much U.S. officials wanted to declare themselves powerless to stop the bloodshed in the former Portuguese colony, they still found it harder to justify their "helpless indignation," whether by deferring to the UN or calling on the Indonesian armed forces to ensure the safety of the same people they had so brutally oppressed for twenty-five years. Though clearly determined to ward off the proliferation of so-called humanitarian interventions and ethical wars, the Clinton administration realized that it could no longer rely on the same arguments as before Allied Force. At least, its representatives could not expect to get away with claiming that the United States was not meant to endorse the role of "world policeman," that the responsibility for preventing "civil" violence in East Timor lay primarily with the Indonesian army, and that an international intervention should be incumbent on the UN Security Council's authorization.[21] Though U.S. officials still tried to resort to these very arguments, they were rapidly dissuaded by the scores of articles and editorials reminding them that in the spring of 1999, the president himself had: given precedence to "a hopeful affirmation of human dignity and human rights" over the territorial integrity of a recognized nation-state; granted "democracies" the right to prevent "evil and aggression" without a UN mandate; and diagnosed massive and organized deportation as the deliberate and systematic implementation of a political agenda rather than the consequence of a chaotic civil war.

While defending their response to Milosevic's unexpected defiance impelled the U.S. government and its allies to adopt —however temporarily—the overly demanding posture of liberal crusaders, symmetrically, opposing Allied Force put a progressive mouthpiece such as the *Nation* in the position of championing causes and institutions that one would not normally associate with an anti-imperialist agenda. In particular, as of late March 1999, the leftist weekly suddenly displayed a surprising attachment to the principle of national sovereignty and an unprecedented respect for the authority of the UN Security Council. Whereas the defective arguments listed earlier provided the best rhetorical formulas—"Give peace a chance," "Two wrongs don't make a right," "Why Kosovo and not Kurdistan, Palestine, or Tibet?" and so on— in terms of substance, the leftist case against the operation relied primarily on the blatant illegality of NATO's air campaign.[22] The sponsors of the undeclared war against Serbia were not only accused of violating the UN Charter—according to article 2(7), "Matters which are essentially within the domestic jurisdiction of any state" are not subject to international interventions—but more important, of deliberately ignoring the Security Council—whose power to declare any conflict a "threat to international peace and security" constitutes the only legal challenge to state sovereignty.

In March 1999, Western leaders knew that both Russia and China would veto any resolution involving even the slightest infringement of Belgrade's "domestic jurisdiction."[23] They thus decided to bypass the Security Council altogether, thereby exposing themselves to the charge of having secured NATO's credibility at the expense of UN authority. To this charge, advocates of military action against Serbia replied that a "humanitarian intervention" such as operation Allied Force, while taking liberties with the charter, was finally giving some teeth to the other major document produced under the aegis of the UN, namely, the Universal Declaration of Human Rights. For the *Nation* editors, however, the decision to mount a so-called humanitarian intervention, though not objectionable in itself, could not be left to the discretion of Western governments alone. Accordingly, they chose to defend the rights of "poor" heads of state against the imperial arrogance of their rich and powerful counterparts rather than condone the latter's license to exercise their selective concern for human rights on behalf of the former's victims. This amounted to reclaiming a position that anti-imperialist activists had held throughout the age of decolonization — that is, from the end of World War II to the early 1960s — but gradually abandoned as the antiauthoritarian revolts of the late 1960s and antitotalitarian sensibility of the late 1970s — in the wake of the Helsinki Agreements — chipped away at their solidarity with the "progressive" governments of the Second and Third Worlds. Yet this time around, invoking the principle of national sovereignty and reserving to the Security Council the privilege of suspending it were bound to have different implications than during the heroic days of national liberation movements — even if these stances were still meant to deny Western powers the right to mount punitive military operations unilaterally.

No matter how much progressive venues such as the *Nation* enjoy recycling old slogans — "hands off Vietnam" can easily be turned into "hands off Iraq" or "hands off Yugoslavia" — the comfort they will get from rousing familiar sentiments and refurbishing a time-honored rhetoric risks being more than offset by the disquieting consequences of pleading for the "rogue states" and other "renegade regimes" that are likely to be the victims of future Western aggressions. Indeed, for the representatives of the anti-imperialist Left, the main trouble with the post–cold war period is that the foes of the West can no longer be perceived as friends. In that respect, the unsavory nature of the Iraqi regime already proved a nagging annoyance for much of the progressive opposition to the Gulf War. But challenging Western hegemony with a promising alternative—at least in terms of human and political rights—appeared even more problematic in the wake of NATO's air campaign against Serbia, since the detractors of operation Allied Force could not convincingly argue that a world where the United States had kept its hands off Kosovo would be a better place.[24]

Therefore, insofar as Western military imperialism continues to target regimes whose patriotic resistance to the U.S.-led new world order primarily consists of oppressing, deporting, or exterminating minorities, the *Nation* editors may find it increasingly taxing to condemn humanitarian interventions modeled on Allied Force. For even if they manage to demonstrate that crude interests, such as access to oil or the credibility of a military alliance, are the real reasons behind the next so-called ethical war, chances are that the violations of human rights that a Western coalition will use as a pretext for resorting to force will be real enough. Consequently, many readers of anti-imperialist publications—at least those who recognize that preventing genocide and ethnic cleansing are causes worthy of the Left—might consider that the situation on the ground warrants a military intervention, regardless of whether intervening powers harbor ulterior motives, violate state sovereignty, or even act without a UN mandate.

Further damage could be caused to the position developed by the *Nation* in response to NATO's intervention in Kosovo if the precedent created by Allied Force were to pressure Western powers into mounting a military operation against a regime that they previously supported but whose policies had been denounced by the anti-imperialist Left. On the one hand, the latter would not want—or at least dare—to subordinate one of its longstanding causes to its newfound attachment to the Security Council as the sole arbiter of international legality. Symmetrically, progressives could not go as far as turning their own traditional foes into friends just because the West was now turning against them. Yet on the other hand, having condemned the use of force against Serbia, leftist critics of democracies' self-assigned duty to prevent evil and aggression would not be in a position to cite Clinton and Blair's proclamations about what they had done in Kosovo as an argument in favor of intervention elsewhere.

Far from hypothetical, such an eventuality materialized less than three months after NATO forces entered Kosovo when the results of the referendum organized by the UN in East Timor prompted the Indonesian military and their paramilitary adjuncts to launch a well-prepared campaign against the population of the former Portuguese colony.[25] Occupied by Indonesia in 1975 with the full support of the United States, East Timor had been the site of some of the worst atrocities committed in the name of the Free World, and thus represented a major cause for the anti-imperialist Left.[26] However, the latter's stance on Kosovo could not help but muddle its protest when both the UN and Western governments initially tried to call themselves powerless to stop the reign of terror that followed the referendum on East Timor's future status.

While liberal commentators and human rights activists who had advocated military action against Serbia could now flood the mainstream press with articles and editorials claiming that Western leaders were bound by their recent commitments to intervene in East Timor—regardless of whether they received an invitation from the Indonesian government or a mandate from the Security Council—for their part, the leftist detractors of operation Allied Force were in no position to demand that "democracies" ignore a possible Chinese veto and send troops to save the East Timorese population. The best a publication such as the *Nation* could do was first to remind its readers of U.S. complicity in the East Timorese tragedy, and then ask President Clinton to "make clear that Indonesian military assistance and World Bank credits are ended . . . until East Timor is free."[27] The weakness of the *Nation*'s case was further underscored by the fact that the relentless stressing by liberal and human rights activists of the parallel between Kosovo and East Timor eventually turned out to be effective: rightly or wrongly, U.S., British, and French leaders felt that after their high-minded speeches of June, public opinion would not let them get away with helpless indignation in September. In turn, both the secretary general and the two other permanent members of the Security Council, because they did not want to risk being sidelined once again, responded to the Kosovo precedent by authorizing an international intervention in East Timor and endowing it with peacemaking powers.

If what happened to the Kosovars and East Timorese in 1999 is indicative of conflicts to come, both the *Nation* and U.S. administration are likely to regret the symmetrical discursive shifts that NATO's intervention in Kosovo inspired in them. Indeed, if a sizable portion of regional wars continue to involve regimes intent on using genocide or deportation to either mobilize patriotic sentiments in their favor or at least give a sense of purpose to their own armed forces, then officially championing democracies' responsibility to fight for human dignity and human rights will prove ever more burdensome for Western governments, whereas defending the inviolability of national sovereignty and the privileges of the Security Council will become increasingly embarrassing for the anti-imperialist Left.

Furthermore, from a political point of view, the commitments made by Western leaders to prevent evil and aggression will considerably heighten their exposure to the pressures of human rights groups, humanitarian organizations, and other proselytizing liberals, while progressive objections to unilateral humanitarian interventions will sound uncomfortably similar to the positions held by the isolationist Right in the United States and the various brands of nationalist parties in Europe.[28] On the one hand, because of pronouncements such as Clinton's victory speech in June 1999 and Blair's reference to Allied Force as an ethical war, liberal activists will be in a better position to demand that U.S. and European officials finally make good on the liberal promise of the late 1980s—namely, that the defeat of communism be turned into a victory for the democratic rule of law, not simply the hegemony of the market.[29] On the other hand, because of their stance on NATO's air campaign in Kosovo, anti-imperialist venues such as the *Nation* will have a hard time distinguishing their arguments from the isolationist—and European nationalist—contention that state sovereignty is the only antidote to the twin ills of the global age: free trade and humanitarian interventionism.[30]

Burdened by cumbersome causes and vulnerable to the latter's natural supporters, the U.S. government and its progressive critics would probably be equally relieved if they could turn the clock back, discursively at least, to the period preceding NATO's intervention in Kosovo. In contrast, both the advocates of a proactive liberal globalization—who expect Western democracies to lobby as aggressively for human rights and civil liberties as for open markets and unchecked capital flows—and the defenders of sovereign nation-states—who stand for the right of national governments to resist the political and economic dictates of foreign powers and international institutions—can only welcome the prospect of a resurgent ideological divide based on their respective agendas.

As the first test of the new political and moral discourse that accompanied NATO's intervention in Kosovo, the resolution of the East Timorese crisis gave considerable credibility to this emerging political polarization between the champions of global liberalism and the protectors of state sovereignty. Barely a few weeks later, however, the reaction of Western leaders to the launching of the second Chechen war by the beleaguered government of Boris Yeltsin demonstrated the fragility of the precedent created by Allied Force.[31] Indeed, in the last weeks of October 1999, as Russian artillery, missiles, and warplanes were savagely and indiscriminately pounding the entire Chechen territory, representatives of the international community did not even go as far as responding with helpless indignation to the fact that several hundred thousand Chechen civilians were driven from their destroyed homes toward the borders of Ingushetia—an autonomous republic of the Russian Federation—and Georgia.

In sharp contrast to their June proclamations about the unacceptability of massive and systematic deportation, U.S. and European officials refrained from either challenging the right of their Russian counterparts to handle the Chechen issue as they pleased or even officially questioning Moscow's claim that fighting "international terrorism" was the motive behind Russia's intervention in Chechnya. In spite of the peace settlement signed by the Yeltsin administration with the Chechen authorities in 1996, the democratic election of Aslan Maskhadov as President of Chechnya in 1997—an election conducted under the supervision of the Organization for Security and Cooperation in Europe (OSCE)—and the alleged commitment of Western democracies to prevent evil and aggression even within the borders of a sovereign state, Western leaders unanimously agreed with the Russian government that Chechnya was part of Russia and no one was entitled to meddle in Russia's internal affairs. Though humanitarian and human rights organizations such as Doctors of the World and Human Rights Watch were rapidly able to gather indisputable evidence that the crimes committed by Russian troops were of the same nature and magnitude as those perpetrated by Serbian forces in Kosovo and the pro-Indonesian militias in East Timor, officials in Washington, London, and Paris merely expressed concern for the fate of the noncombatants caught in the fighting. They thus respectfully asked Russian troops to refrain from using disproportionate force, to keep the border between Chechnya and Ingushetia open for refugees, and to give the latter access to international humanitarian aid.

For anyone who wished that the proclamations surrounding operation Allied Force would constitute an irreversible doctrinal shift, the reaction of Western governments to the second war in Chechnya was distressing on two counts. First, the similarities between Yeltsin's campaign against Chechnya and Milosevic's plans for Kosovo were rather striking. They involved the context of the Russian decision to wage an all-out war against the Chechens—more precisely, the attempt by a faltering and corrupt government to regain the public's favor by fueling nationalist and racist sentiments; the pretext used by the Russian government for invading Chechnya—that is, the necessity to fight "Islamic terrorism"; and the true objective of the war—the old project, successively taken on by the czars and Joseph Stalin, of emptying Chechnya of its Chechen population. Second, to prevent the Yeltsin government from prolonging its murderous campaign, Western governments could resort to the same means that had just proved efficient with the Indonesian authorities. In other words, to deter Russian officials from emulating their colleagues in Belgrade, there was obviously no need to either threaten Moscow with another NATO operation or even offer military assistance to the Chechen army. Considering both the disastrous financial situation of the Russian Federation and the responsibility of the Yeltsin clan in the bankruptcy of the country, the ailing president and his latest prime minister, former KGB officer Vladimir Putin, were hardly in a position to ignore a simple statement by the International Monetary Fund (IMF) and its Western sponsors announcing that loans to Russia would be subordinated to the withdrawal of Russian troops from Chechnya and the resumption of the dialogue between Russian authorities and the Maskhadov government.

Ostensibly offended by Moscow's methods in the first months of the second Chechen war, Western governments all but withheld their criticism of Russia once Yeltsin resigned in favor of Putin and Russian troops reduced the Chechen capital Grozny to rubble. Despite accumulating evidence of massive human rights violations, both in the regions of Chechnya under Moscow's control and in the so-called "filtration camps" set up by the Russian army in Ingushetia, the OSCE did not even sanction Moscow, let alone suspend Russia's membership for as long as its government would violate its charter. As for Clinton and Blair, they unequivocally embraced Putin as their candidate for the Russian presidential elections of March 2000. On February 14, 2000, less than eight months after proclaiming democracies' duty to fight evil and aggression, the U.S. president declared on CNN that Russia's acting president was a man "that the United States can do business with." Following Clinton's lead, the British prime minister who had portrayed NATO's intervention in Kosovo as an ethical war paid a friendly visit to Putin on March 11, 2000 — two weeks before election day — and called for "a closer partnership between the European Union and Russia." Although both leaders continued to ask that Russian troops use more restraint vis-à-vis Chechen civilians, their more than implicit endorsement of Yeltsin's successor amounted to supporting the systematic destruction of Chechnya, since the latter was both the main tenet of Putin's platform and the only reason for his popularity among the Russian population.

To justify their extraordinary leniency toward the new Russian administration, U.S. and European officials could count on a seasoned rhetoric: minor adjustments notwithstanding, they simply refurbished the same arguments they had already resorted to prior to March 1999 with respect to Milosevic and his allies. First, Western governments insisted that maintaining a cordial dialogue with Moscow gave them a better chance of convincing the Russian authorities to minimize the suffering inflicted on Chechen civilians. Similarly, during the Bosnian War, the representatives of the international community had contended that antagonizing Bosnian Serb militias would only worsen the plight of their victims. Second, to explain their endorsement of a man who was waging a brutal colonial war in order to win a presidential election, Western officials claimed that they had no other choice, since a Putin administration was the least anti-Western option for Russia, and thus, the most likely to be open to humanitarian concerns. As already mentioned, from Dayton to Rambouillet, U.S. and European diplomats had also argued that however offensive, Milosevic was nonetheless the best buffer against a "truly" extremist brand of Serbian nationalism. Third, to defend their low profile on the political aspects of the Chechen war, Western leaders stressed that the complex and volatile character of the Caucasian region called for extreme caution on their part. There again, from 1991 to 1999, the explosive nature of the Balkans had been raised as a reason against acting too harshly on behalf of the Bosnians and Kosovars. Finally, the U.S. president and his European counterparts conveyed that regardless of the lot of the Chechen people, angering a nuclear power on a hazardous road to democracy could only be counterproductive—especially at a time when arms control negotiations were in a difficult phase. Though for its part, Serbia never had any nuclear weapons, one of the main reasons proffered by UN and Western diplomats for not confronting the ethnic cleansers in Bosnia and Kosovo had been that a military intervention against Serbia would impel Russia and its nuclear arsenal to come to the rescue of its traditional ally.

The return, in the winter of 2000, of the rhetoric that had dominated most of the 1990s was met with little public protest in Western countries, especially in the United States. For radical militants as well as liberal activists—the two constituencies most likely to express outrage—the solicitude of the West for Putin's Russia proved just too difficult to address. For the members of the anti-imperialist Left, there was no way of reconciling Clinton and Blair's conciliatory attitude toward Russia's dirty war with their own contention that the new hegemonic strategy of the West—that is, what Noam Chomsky calls the "new military humanism"—consists of manipulating the noble causes of human rights and humanitarianism in order to bypass international law and degrade the sovereignty of non-Western nations. As for liberals, most of them were still too proud of their leaders' commitment to stop evil and aggression, and thus, unwilling to reckon with the obvious contradiction between Western responses to the cleansing of Kosovo and the destruction of Chechnya.

While it may be too early to assess whether the discursive shifts that surrounded operation Allied Force will be completely reversed, what Western reactions to the Chechen crisis already call for is an analysis of the rhetoric after which they are fashioned. In other words, what still needs to be examined is the discourse that U.S. and European officials applied to post–cold war conflicts before the launching of NATO's air campaign against Serbia. Elaborated in the wake of the Gulf War, this remarkable rhetoric saved Western leaders from addressing the ethnic cleansing of Bosnia and Rwandan genocide in the way that they eventually had to deal with Kosovo. Consequently, it also spared the anti-imperialist Left the embarrassment of mirroring the isolationist Right, and deprived both the supporters of a liberal globalization and the uphold-ers of state sovereignty of an ideological divide ostensibly informed by the tension between the Universal Declaration of Human Rights and article 2(7) of the UN Charter.

As already mentioned with regard to Bosnia, this discourse was based on the claim that the sudden resurgence of ancient enmities, rather than the implementation of a current political project, was the primary cause of post–cold war conflicts. Accordingly, solving the latter did not call for democracies invested with a duty to mobilize and possibly mount humanitarian interventions against evil and aggressive regimes but for a so-called international community whose responsibilities included mediating between rival factions steeped in ancestral hatreds, bringing humanitarian assistance to the civilian victims of these age-old disputes, and interrupting the cycles of vengeance and retribution by fostering peace, stability, and the establishment of the rule of law. Therefore, whether NATO's intervention in Kosovo has actually marked a turning point in the management of post–cold war conflicts—for Western governments themselves; for their radical, liberal, and isolationist critics; and most important, for the protagonists of these conflicts—will largely depend on how much damage it has done to the "doctrine of the international community."

A New Doctrine

The late 1980s was a time of great liberal expectations. As the cold war was coming to an end, U.S. and Western European liberals were convinced that history was finally vindicating their cause. Thrilled by the peaceful revolutions in Eastern Europe, they expected the peoples who were liberating themselves from Communist oppression to embrace liberal democracy with passion and zeal. Such wholehearted enthusiasm, they believed, would not only humble the remnants of the old anti-imperialist Left in the West but also rejuvenate the democratic faith of all jaded Westerners. Moreover, Western liberals assumed that with the waning of the Soviet threat, their own governments would no longer be able to justify their support of anticommunist dictators in the developing world. "Authoritarian" regimes having become as obsolete as their "totalitarian" counterparts—to use a distinction dear to the Reagan administration—liberals could envision the 1990s as a promising period of transition toward worldwide democracy.

During the ten years spanning the fall of the Berlin Wall to NATO's intervention in Kosovo, these liberal expectations would know a paradoxical fate. On the one hand, Western governments ostensibly identified with them. Indeed, leaders in the United States and Europe proudly associated the end of the cold war with the advent of an increasingly cohesive international community whose concerns extended beyond the tasks of maintaining peace and seeking stability in all regions of the world. According to its Western sponsors, the new international community was also committed to fostering democracy and preventing human rights violations, even when the latter were perpetrated by the agents of a recognized state against their own population. But on the other hand, the international community of the 1990s failed to avert the genocide of the Tutsis in Rwanda and the ethnic cleansing campaigns launched by the Serbian regime in the former Yugoslavia; furthermore, it hardly fared any better in dealing with the use of famine as a form of warfare in Sudan, the systematic slaughter of civilians in Algeria, Russia's brutal reaction to Chechnya's declaration of independence, the civil wars that devastated Liberia, Somalia, and Burundi, and the reigns of terror imposed by the rebels in Sierra Leone and the Taliban in Afghanistan—to name only a fraction of the most revolting episodes of the decade.

At the heart of this apparent discrepancy between discourse and reality lies the deceptively familiar entity known as the international community. While already delineated in documents such as the UN Charter of 1945, the Universal Declaration of Human Rights of 1948, the Genocide Convention of 1948, the Geneva Conventions of 1949, the International Covenant on Civil and Political Rights of 1966, and the Convention against Torture of 1984, the international community was nonetheless considered a purely virtual entity throughout the cold war. Conversely, as soon as the paralyzing rivalry between the two former superpowers came to an end, a wide variety of voices announced the imminent emergence of an actual international community bound by the same rules of international law and represented by authoritative international institutions. Western leaders applauded this prospect as the felicitous consequence of their victory, UN officials celebrated it as a new dawn for their organization, outgoing Soviet and incoming Russian diplomats affected to embrace what they described as a new era of cooperation, and even the Chinese government welcomed the advent of a community of nations whose guiding principle would be a revamped respect for the national sovereignty of all its members.

If the UN peacekeeping mission to Namibia in 1989 can probably be identified as the inaugural act of the new age, the first defining moment for the emerging international community was undeniably the Gulf War. Between January 17 and February 28, 1991, George Bush and Margaret Thatcher managed to conduct their war against Iraq under the aegis of the UN and with the assistance of a vast number of states—some of which were not even traditional clients of the West. Thus, not only could the U.S. president and British prime minster claim that a "new world order" was under way but also that it was implemented in the name of an undivided international community. Yet, both the content of this new world order and the status of the international community sanctioning it were immediately subject to diverging interpretations.

For the detractors of operation Desert Storm, whether in the Arab world or among the Western Left, what the new world order stood for was easy to understand. It meant that the collapse of the Soviet bloc had given the U.S. government —with the help of its allies and clients—an unprecedented opportunity to secure the economic and cultural hegemony of Western capitalism. Accordingly, anti-imperalist critics interpreted the international community hailed by Western powers as nothing more than a newfound alibi. In their view, the fact that the war against Iraq was waged in the name of a so-called international community merely conveyed that the victors of the cold war were now able to bribe their former rivals and pressure the United Nations into granting them the legal authorization to pursue their crude interests as, when, and where they saw fit.

For the sponsors of the Gulf War, however, defining the new world order and its relationship with the international community proved considerably more complicated. During the months leading to Desert Storm, Bush offered two main reasons for not letting Hussein get away with the annexation of Kuwait. On the one side, for the sake of his European allies and the "internationalist" wing of his party, he claimed that invading a sovereign country was exactly the kind of violation of international law that the new world order could no longer tolerate. On the other side, the president warned his more isolationist constituents that allowing the Iraqi leader to become the dominant player in the Persian Gulf presented both a mortal danger to Iraq's neighbors—especially those who were friends with the United States—and a major threat to U.S. vital interests.[32] As the deadline given to Hussein for pulling out his troops grew closer, though, the U.S. government and its British ally were confronted with the persistent lack of enthusiasm shown by the Western public at the prospect of liberating Kuwait. Desperate to increase the approval rate for their imminent campaign, they thus decided to proclaim, rather cavalierly, that intervening in the gulf would also serve the cause of democracy, in Kuwait as well as Iraq. In other words, the national security of Western powers and their fresh determination to defend the national sovereignty of a recognized state no longer were the only motives that would justify a war against Iraq: according to U.S. and European officials, forcing Hussein's troops out of Kuwait was also supposed to foster the major political hope raised by the outcome of the cold war, namely, the impending demise of all undemocratic regimes.

This new, and probably improvised, line of reasoning briefly occupied center stage on February 15, 1991—about a month into the war—when Bush addressed the Iraqi people directly, calling on them "to take matters into their own hands and force Saddam Hussein, the dictator, to step aside." When Kurdish and Shia insurgents took Bush's words seriously enough to attempt overthrowing "Saddam Hussein, the dictator," however, the U.S. president not only refused to give them any help but even denied having ever prompted their revolt.[33] What motivated this quick reversal was the realization among U.S. officials that promoting democracy in the Persian Gulf, or even persuasively claiming to do so, was incompatible with pursuing American interests in the region—such as ensuring an abundant and cheap oil supply, securing the stability of friendly regimes, and preventing the modification of internationally recognized borders.

First, the Bush administration feared that a successful Shia insurgency in the south of Iraq would strengthen Iran, which remained the principal foe of the United States in the Middle East. As well, U.S. officials were convinced that they could not support the rebellion of the Iraqi Kurds in the north of the country without risking the breakup of Iraq, and also raising the anxiety of the Turkish government—a friend of the United States, a member of NATO, and another oppressor of Kurds—regarding a united and independent Kurdistan. Third, by seriously advocating democratization in Iraq and Kuwait, Washington was bound to anger its most important yet most antidemocratic ally in the region, Saudi Arabia. For all these reasons, the "reasonable" thing to do was to allow Hussein to remain in power long enough to preserve the territorial integrity of Iraq, and then hope for a coup by his entourage that would replace the dictator without altering the dictatorship.[34] But if such "reason" were to prevail, what was left of the trumpeted connection between the new world order and the advancement of an international community committed to liberal democracy and human rights?

The appellation "new world order" did not survive the double reinstatement of Hussein's rule and the Kuwaiti old regime—until it was revived, in 1999, by the detractors of NATO's intervention in Kosovo. In contrast, the expression "international community" found its true raison d'être, or at least the doctrine to which it would be attached for the next eight years, in the aftermath of the Gulf War. In the early days of April 1991, as CNN broadcast how Iraqi troops were crushing the Kurdish rebellion that Bush had so recklessly encouraged—thereby forcing about two million Iraqi Kurds to flee toward the Turkish border—the Western sponsors of Desert Storm realized that having called Hussein a new Hitler, they could not stand by while the Iraqi leader acted in a Hitler fashion without damaging their own credibility. They thus decided to launch operation "Provide Comfort," which consisted of successively bringing humanitarian assistance to the refugees, committing U.S. troops to allow them to return to their homes, and even establishing Iraqi Kurdistan as a permanent "safe haven"—though still officially within Iraq—protected from Hussein's vengeance by U.S. warplanes based in Turkey.

Insofar as the Bush administration and its European allies failed to combine the words *humanitarian* and *impartial*, the way in which they defended their decision to intervene in Iraq proper was not yet the model of what would become the rhetoric of the international community. Still, the discourse supporting operation Provide Comfort already summoned up the three different communities that the phrase "international community" would henceforth be associated with. The first of these communities had no agency of its own and was therefore largely putative: it joined individuals—mostly cable television viewers—from all over the world, who despite the cultural differences between them, were expected to show the same feelings of compassion and outrage in the face of massive suffering—whether caused by natural disasters or human violence—and would thus demand that competent institutions act to rescue the surviving victims. But at the same time, international community also referred to a society of independent nation-states, whose legitimate claims to political sovereignty and territorial integrity could sometimes clash with international relief operations—especially when the perpetrators and victims of the human suffering deemed intolerable by the international community of compassionate individuals would respectively be the legal authorities of a recognized state and a population under their jurisdiction. Finally, the third entity conjured up was the global citizenry in progress, whose advent was to follow from the outcome of the cold war. According to its harbingers, this international community of citizens would result from the gradual conversion of all nations to the democratic rule of law, and hence, the reconciliation of every government's claim to national sovereignty with the humanitarian aspirations of the people it governs.

That the three acceptations of the phrase did not have a common referent was precisely what enabled Western governments to act as the legitimate representatives of the international community. To begin with, by virtue of their economic and military power, the United States and its European allies were clearly the leading members of the society of nations; second, they were identified with the humanitarian aspirations of the world public—aspirations, primarily nurtured by the Western media, that only Western powers had the material means to fulfill; and lastly, as victors of the cold war, they were officially committed to the advancement of a global democratic citizenry since they had presented it as the outcome of their victory itself. Western authorities could there-

37

fore assign themselves the goal of supplying the missing referent to the international community and define their specific role as that of a temporary surrogate. As such, they presented the accomplishment of their mission as a balancing act between the various international communities that they purported to represent. They were, in other words, to respond to humanitarian emergencies while respecting the protocols of international relations, yet not let the latter prevail over the prospect of global democratization.

Rhetorically, these conflicting responsibilites enabled the leading members of the international community to persuade their constituents of the extreme difficulty of their task. Practically, however, the diverging requirements enveloped in the phrase "international community" gave some remarkable leeway to its self-assigned representatives. Indeed, according to whether Western governments wanted to minimize, limit, or maximize their involvement in a conflict, they could respectively hide behind the iron rule of national sovereignty and defer to the diplomatic skills of UN officials; underscore the necessity of alleviating human suffering and impose that relief organizations gain access to the victims; or raise the cause of human rights and take it into their own hands to implement the rule of law.

In the aftermath of the Gulf War, a growing number of conflicts involved either the sudden collapse of cold war dictatorships—such as Samuel Doe's Liberia and Siad Barre's Somalia—or conversely, their monstrous resistance—as in the cases of Milosevic's Yugoslavia and Juvénal Habyarimana's Rwanda. Although the level of extreme violence that these conflicts generated threatened to ridicule the very notion of an international community, Western officials continued to assert that the ultimate objective of their mission consisted of facilitating the transition to democracy for every society that was either emerging from civil war or throwing off the fetters of authoritarian rule. In order to maintain the credibility of their claim, the representatives of the international community drew on the ambiguities of their self-assigned position to develop a doctrine that was radically at odds with the prevailing policies of the cold war era.

Between the end of World War II and the late 1980s, Western governments and their Communist rivals had systematically projected their own competition onto every conflict. Regardless of the actual practices of the local players, both Washington and Moscow spent about forty-five years investing virtually all civil insurgencies and regional crises with an ideological content that called for their own partisan participation. Consequently, their assessment of these conflicts largely depended on the political allegiance of the parties involved: Western governments denounced Communist dictators and guerrillas but mainly covered up—and even sponsored—the abuses committed by their own protégés, while socialist regimes condemned the crimes of anticommunist dictators and rebels but concealed their own.

In stark contrast with their predecessors' biases, the Western governments that now acted as the leading members of the new and potentially united international community no longer envisioned local conflicts in terms of ideological persuasion and political allegiance. Although the United States and, to a lesser extent, its European allies still had official enemies—leaders of so-called rogue states who sheltered and funded terrorist organizations—these foes tended to be treated as international outlaws rather than the exponents of a rival political agenda. But as far as local conflicts were concerned, unless they were fomented by a rogue state, the policy of the international community was to deny them any relevant ideological content. Even if they had started during the cold war—and were then interpreted in terms of the competition between the Free World and communism—their motives were now attributed to cultural, or even personal, enmities rather than meaningful political antagonisms.

Indeed, throughout most of the 1990s, virtually all local conflicts were officially attributed to a combination of two causes: the existence of old and intractable "bad blood" between neighboring or intertwined communities, and the exploitation of these ingrained feelings by ruthless warlords. Although the relative importance of cultural resentment and personal ambitions varied from one conflict to another, the leading members of the international community contended that all post–cold war conflicts were about "tribal" disputes — over land, resources, ethnic or religious supremacy, and so forth — rather than rival ideologies and adverse political projects. Therefore, they believed that their own intervention in these conflicts had to be, or at least appear to be, nonpartisan. Confronted with what they described as purely sectarian struggles, they did not want to be perceived as either siding with a party, condoning violence, or even wishing for someone's victory. To the contrary, the aim of the international community was to appear as the unconditional protector of all civilian victims, the impartial agent of peace, the zealot of the rule of law, and the promoter of reconciliation. Consequently, what can be called the doctrine of the international community unfolded as follows:

> 1. The representatives of the international community proclaimed that their primary concern was the fate of the civilian victims of local conflicts. Their first objective was thus to bring humanitarian aid to civilian populations on both sides of the frontlines, but also to impose the presence of relief agencies — either protected by peacekeepers or at least accompanied by Western journalists and international monitors — as a preliminary step toward the cessation of hostilities.

2. The representatives conceived of their diplomatic mission as that of a proactive yet impartial mediator between warring factions. As such, their role was first to pressure the faction leaders into declaring a truce and looking for a negotiated settlement, then to sponsor and arbitrate the peace process until an agreement was reached, and finally, to guarantee that all parties abide by the treaty they had signed.

3. Once the negotiations were in motion, the political aspect of the international community's intervention consisted of committing the formerly warring parties to the reinstatement, or establishment, of the rule of law. Various international agencies would thus condition both their economic assistance and military protection on the creation of democratic institutions—either within pre-existing borders or in the new entities defined by the peace treaty—and the organization of free and fair elections.

4. The international community representatives claimed that their ultimate goal was to promote reconciliation not only between the warring factions themselves but, more important, between their respective communities. To this end, and as evidence of the reinstated rule of law, they demanded that the perpetrators of war crimes and crimes against humanity be held individually accountable for their actions—hence the creation of ad hoc international war crimes tribunals and, eventually, the permanent International Criminal Court—but also that justice be exercised in a way that served mutual forgiveness and warded off collective vengeance.

Although they did not appear particularly proud of their record, especially in places like Bosnia and Rwanda, the leading members of the international community stood firmly by the principles that informed their doctrine. Neither indifferent to human tragedies nor driven by imperialist motives, they argued that they had no other design than to provide humanitarian relief, call for dialogue rather than violence, foster social and economic recovery, advance democratic institutions, and enable the victims of horrendous crimes to bring their legitimate claims to justice. In other words, the Western leaders who dictated the agenda of the international community likened their own motivations to the purposes of popular nongovernmental organizations (NGOs) such as humanitarian agencies and human rights groups. If some of them conceded that during the crises of the early 1990s, they should have intervened more promptly and forcefully, even the most apologetic contended that their mode of intervention was faithful to the social ideals promoted by the end of the cold war—namely, humanitarianism, democracy, and universal human rights.

Though it proved coherent and operative, the doctrine of the international community did not result from a concerted plan secretly devised by U.S. officials and their European allies. Rather, the formation of this doctrine resembled its eventual crisis, in the spring of 1999, in that it consisted less of the implementation of a deliberate strategy than a mix of trials and errors, hasty decisions, and hindsight rationalizations. Furthermore, the fact that the language of the international community was spoken by all its representatives did not mean that the latter necessarily shared the same interests. Quite to the contrary, part of what made the doctrine successful was that it not only enabled its authorized users to funnel their sometimes competing agendas through it but also allowed them to blame each other for the often wanting record of the international community. For instance, the U.S. government frequently imputed the protractedness of post–cold war conflicts to the excessive propensity of its European counterparts—especially the French—to compromise with the warring parties, whereas European authorities complained relentlessly about the contrast between the righteous discourse and isolationist practices of their U.S. allies. There again, the constant bickering that went on among Western governments was neither the proof of concerted planning nor a reason to call into question the reality of the international community, but a contingent factor that nonetheless contributed to the efficacy of the discourse proffered in the name of the international community.

Historically, the doctrine came about as the result of a gradual and somewhat piecemeal process. First, as already mentioned, the very notion of an international community committed to bringing the world under the rule of law appeared at the outset of the Gulf War. International community was indeed the name given by Bush and Thatcher to the coalition that was to liberate Kuwait, and defending the rule of law and fostering democracy were among the alleged purposes of this new entity. The way in which the incipient international community endeavored to fulfill its self-assigned mission, however—namely, a military intervention against a head of state who had violated the new world order—is precisely what the subsequent developments of the doctrine purported to avoid. Until NATO's intervention in Kosovo, the Gulf War was thus the last international conflict where, in good cold war style, Western governments and their supporters acted as "hawks," while their left-leaning critics played the traditional role of the pacifist "doves."

Second, the concept of a humanitarian intervention sponsored by the international community can be traced to operations Provide Comfort and "Restore Hope": while the former purported to shelter the Kurds of northern Iraq from Hussein's immediate reaction to the Gulf War, the latter was supposed to protect the Somalian civilians from the warlords who were accused of destroying their country. Although they both received the humanitarian label, as far as the doctrine in progress was concerned, the Somalian intervention represented a clear evolution. Whereas Provide Comfort was still confrontational, insofar as its goal was to stave off an aggression planned by a political regime, Restore Hope was originally meant to bring relief to the Somalian population while not taking sides in the power struggle between the various factions. Restore Hope, in other words, should be credited with having established the equivalence between the terms *humanitarian* and *impartial*—even if its U.S. sponsors eventually singled out the militias of General Mohammed Aideed as the main obstacle to their mission. Therefore, despite its dismal outcome, operation Restore Hope can be defined as the prototypical humanitarian mission of the post–cold war era.

Third, the idea that the international community should operate as a forceful though neutral mediator between warring parties was first applied to resolve conflicts that had begun during the cold war—such as the civil wars in Mozambique, Angola, Guatemala, and El Salvador—but had lost their ideological meaning with the demise of the Communist empire. Once the Angolan regime and Salvadoran guerrillas ceased to be associated with the Soviet menace, for instance, the U.S. government no longer felt inclined to either turn the soldiers of Jonas Savimbi's National Union for the Total Independence of Angola (UNITA) into worthy "freedom fighters" on the CIA payroll, or fund the Salvadoran regime and its death squads. Instead, Washington joined other eminent members of the international community in their project to organize and mediate peace conferences that would end the violence and prompt reconciliation between what was now perceived as equally representative, and even legitimate, warring parties.

Fourth, the way in which the war crimes tribunals instituted by the international community—during the Bosnian conflict and in the wake of the Rwandan genocide—were to address the relationship between justice and reconciliation was patterned less after the Nuremberg trials, despite frequent references to them, than a model that was established during the Chilean and Argentinean transitions from military dictatorship to democracy. In 1945, Nuremberg magistrates had designed the trials of Nazi criminals with the intention of stigmatizing the National Socialist regime without incriminating the German people collectively. In contrast, both the Chilean Truth Commission and Argentinean courts enforced the principle of individual accountability in order to prevent collective impunity but without denouncing the criminal nature of the military dictatorship of Augusto Pinochet or the junta successively headed by Generals Jorge Videla, Roberto Viola, and Leopoldo Galtieri. Similarly, what Western governments wanted the International War Crimes Tribunals for the former Yugoslavia and Rwanda to do was to prosecute specific human rights violations and their individual perpetrators. At the same time, however, the type of reconciliation that they wished to promote made them reluctant to let the courts incriminate the political regimes that mandated these crimes.[35]

45

While its specific components—humanitarian, diplomatic, political, judicial—evolved from extremely different situations, as an integrated body, the doctrine of the international community was predicated on a generic definition of post-cold war disputes. This definition was originally devised to interpret the so-called ethnic wars in the Balkans and central Africa, namely, the crises leading to the breakup of Yugoslavia—from Kosovo to Slovenia to Croatia to Bosnia, and back to Kosovo—and the civil wars involving the Hutus and Tutsis, in Burundi and especially Rwanda. Local variations notwithstanding, the authorized voices of the international community argued that the common denominator of these post–cold war conflicts was that they could all be traced to pre–cold war causes.

According to Western officials, when the oppressive though relatively stable governments imposed by the cold war began to crumble, the societies affected by this sudden power vacuum experienced both a strong desire to embrace a promising yet unsettling future and a morbid compulsion to repeat a painful yet familiar past. While some of these torn societies managed to implement a more or less peaceful transition to "modernity"—that is, open markets and democracy—others fell prey to an abrupt resurgence of "premodern" sectarianism. Ancient tribal hatreds and fears that had been literally frozen by the ideological divide of the cold war resurfaced with a vengeance, inducing violent outbreaks of ethnic, religious, or interregional clashes. In turn, cynical politicians established, or sometimes maintained, their power by fueling and exploiting the reawakening of age-old resentments among their neighboring or intertwined communities. Drawing on past tragedies, they first blamed each other's groups for being the cause of their own people's enduring difficulties, and then resorted to war as the solution to their people's problems.

Whether defined as ethnic, religious, or regional groups, the "peoples" that the warring factions and their leaders allegedly represented played an ambivalent role in the script promoted by Western officials. On the one hand, as civilian populations engulfed in the horror of war, they were presented as hapless victims, and thus, the main object of the international community's solicitude. On the other hand, these groups were also charged with actually harboring the deeply ingrained feelings of mutual hatred that were at the root of post–cold war conflicts. Therefore, the peoples caught in these wars were considered innocent and worthy of compassion inasmuch as they suffered at the hands of cynical war-

lords, but they were also guilty and in need of "liberal educa-
tion" because the primitive sectarianism that suffused their
culture was the primary cause of their suffering.

Regardless of its accuracy, this assessment of post–cold war
strife served a crucial purpose for the leading members of
the international community: it justified both the humanitarian and diplomatic provisions of their doctrine in the eyes
of a Western public who was learning about these more or
less exotic conflicts through the media. Indeed, what Western
television viewers primarily witnessed was the plight of unspecified civilians—either wounded, frightened, or running
for their lives—and the blind violence displayed by unspecified militias. As such, they could only approve of a humani-   **47**
tarian intervention that purported to offer relief to the former
and protect them from the latter's senseless rage. Yet, at the
same time, whenever the civilian victims of these brutal wars
had a chance to express themselves in the Western media,
they appeared to be plagued by the same sectarian feelings as
their tormentors. In other words, these—usually decontextu-
alized—interviews conveyed that in spite of the damage they
caused, the various factions were nonetheless representative
of the mutual hostility that suffused their respective communities. The Western public could thus only approve of an impartial mediation that sought to broker a truce between the
parties and pressure their leaders into settling their differences through negotiations.

The message that both the humanitarian and diplomatic
missions of the international community meant to convey,
primarily to Western public opinion, was that there were only
two relevant sides in these post–cold war conflicts: the side
of peace, represented by the leaders of the major Western
powers and their empathetic constituents; and the side of war,
composed of all the local factions, regardless of their alleged
motives for fighting. The Western public was invited to re-

gard the parties to these wars as so steeped in old and intractable disputes that weighing their competing claims seemed neither possible nor relevant to the resolution of their conflicts.

While the representatives of the international community recognized that there might be differences in the quantity of crimes and the magnitude of destruction imputable to the various warring parties, they nonetheless maintained that all sides were infected with the same sectarian "bad blood." Given this, they had no reason to make a qualitative distinction between the factions. Rather than either siding with one of the parties or excluding another from the process of political reconstruction, the leading members of the international community professed that the nature of post–cold war conflicts called for a neutral and conciliatory approach. What mattered was not to decide who was right and wrong, since all the factions had committed terrible crimes and all the communities were guilty of harboring heinous feelings, but to persuade all the parties to choose dialogue over violence.

As soon as they met the demands of the international mediators—that is, as soon as they declared a cease-fire and came to the negotiating table—the so-called faction leaders immediately acquired a legitimate place in the process of reconstruction corresponding to the political and judicial provisions of the international community's doctrine. By virtue of their signature on the peace treaty and their solemn commitment to the establishment of the rule of law, they even became the agents of their country's stability and the guardians of its new institutions. As such, and insofar as they refrained from reneging too blatantly, the former faction leaders not only gained access to international aid; they were also supposed to obtain immunity from the international courts investigating war crimes and crimes against humanity.

In principle, the representatives of the international community maintained that a successful process of national reconciliation required everyone to abide by the newly established rule of law. Everyone, in short, should be held accountable for his or her actions. According to the judicial component of the doctrine, enabling the surviving victims of human rights violations to bring their claims to justice not only established the trustworthiness of the new institutions; it was instrumental in moving the entire society toward forgiveness as well. At the same time, however, the representatives of the international community argued that the rule of law could not take hold, and thus could not pave the way for reconciliation, without social and political stability. They conceded that regardless of his or her past record, any local leader committed to the rule of law—and who still had the capacity to disrupt that country's stability—should be protected, at least temporarily, from the scrutiny of international courts.

Though giving priority to stability over justice might seem unprincipled and bound to frustrate victims of wartime abuses, the leading members of the international community contended that their pragmatic approach served the cause of national reconciliation. Moreover, they claimed that the development of a democratic culture would eventually achieve what a less cautious interpretation of justice would only have delivered at the risk of renewed violence. In other words, the representatives of the international community advocated granting immunity to the instigators of post–cold war conflicts in order to avoid the destabilization of societies where these former warlords still held considerable power, but they also professed that democratic elections—which were to follow from the reinstatement of the rule of law—were better suited than international courts for ridding recently pacified societies of their sectarian politicians.

Mostly intended for the Western public, the discursive strategy of the international community included two major statements, respectively pertaining to the etiology of post–cold war disputes and the type of "treatment" that they required. First, these conflicts were attributed to cultural causes, namely, ancestral and intractable feelings of mutual resentment among neighboring or intertwined communities. Although they tended to be exacerbated and exploited by opportunistic and/or fanatic faction leaders, these feelings of ethnic, religious, or interregional hatred were said to be pervasive in all the communities afflicted by these wars. Next, insofar as the representatives of the international community imputed post–cold war strife to a form of cultural backwardness, they necessarily envisioned the resolution of these conflicts in terms of a cultural leap. Therefore, they presented their own mission as both conciliatory and educational: the self-appointed tasks of the international community consisted of pressuring antagonistic communities into forsaking the "rule of blood" while simultaneously educating them in the duties and benefits of the rule of law. Because the transition from civil war to democracy was meant to express a cultural evolution rather than a political verdict, the representatives of the international community argued that they needed to be neutral about the past and privilege stability in the present. That is, they had to put an indiscriminate blame on all the formerly warring factions for having resorted to violence, but also praise and reward them equally for embracing peace and embarking on the road to democracy.

A Radical Critique

Although the 1990s was a time of unprecedented Western hegemony, the harshest critics of the international community and its doctrine were usually not found in neomarxist or pacifist circles. Indeed, the strongest indictment did not come from the radical Left, whose representatives, in Europe and the United States, had relatively little to say about the ethnic cleansing campaign in Bosnia and the Rwandan genocide. For the most part, the people who denounced the doctrine of the international community most stridently were a different breed than the anti-imperialist militants who had mobilized against the Gulf War. They included:

- scholars of the regions caught in post–cold war conflicts whose hackles were raised by the blatant inaccuracy of the ancient hatred explanation;[36]
- members of humanitarian organizations who protested against the abuse of humanitarianism by Western governments;[37]
- war correspondents and essayists reporting for major Western media who witnessed the nefarious effects of the

"impartial mediations" conducted by the international community;[38] and

- human rights activists — associated with Amnesty International, Human Rights Watch, Africa Watch, and others — who accused Western governments of manipulating notions such as stability and reconciliation in order to circumvent their own commitment to the promotion of the rule of law and the principle of individual accountability.

In short, the most emphatic denunciation of the international community did not come from the traditional foes of Western foreign policy but from individuals and organizations whose concerns — that is, humanitarianism, human rights, and the advancement of democracy — Western governments were particularly eager to co-opt.

Obviously, most of these critics did not wait until the end of the cold war to question governmental accounts of local and regional conflicts. In particular, one of the founding purposes of NGOs such as Doctors without Borders and Human Rights Watch was precisely to challenge the partisan logic imposed by the world leaders of the cold war era, on either side of the Iron Curtain.[39] But if the raison d'être of these humanitarian and human rights organizations did not change with the end of the cold war, their problems with Western governments did. While they used to denounce the biases resulting from partisan involvement, their main argument was now with the allegedly nonpartisan rhetoric of the international community. What many reporters, scholars, and nongovernmental activists came to realize throughout the 1990s was that subsuming local disputes under a grand political narrative — such as the struggle against totalitarianism — and reducing them to "prepolitical" tales of tribal hostility were but two equally efficient ways of obfuscating the political stakes of these conflicts. Therefore, the fact that Western governments were now intent on portraying themselves as benign conciliators between antagonistic factions, rather than the contentious champions of the Free World, did not necessarily bode well for the protection of human rights and advancement of democracy.

According to its critics, the official doctrine of the international community was objectionable on four related counts. To begin with, the doctrine was flawed because its premise was false: attributing post–cold war conflicts to cultural causes amounted to obfuscating the political dimensions of these wars. Second, this obfuscation was deliberate. In other words, the leading members of the international community did not simply overlook the political nature of post–cold war hostilities; they chose to deny it in order to serve what they saw as their own political interests. Third, the policies favored by the international community—its humanitarian, diplomatic, political, and judicial interventions—were not only based on a false definition of post–cold war conflicts but actually intended to demonstrate its accuracy. Fourth, the strategy of the international community was unfortunately efficient insofar as it was producing exactly what it purported to fight: thanks to the measures meant to establish its validity, the interpretation of post–cold war disputes in cultural terms tended to become a self-fulfilling prophecy.

Though its relevance is not limited to the wars in the former Yugoslavia and Rwanda, this comprehensive critique primarily applies to the way in which the representatives of the international community reacted both to the ethnic cleansing campaigns launched by the regime of Milosevic and the genocide of the Rwandan Tutsis prepared under the presidency of Habyarimana and executed by his immediate successors. Understandably, the activists, journalists, and scholars who wrote about either of these two situations not only remained

53

site specific but also tended to cautiously confine their criticism of Western policies to their own respective domains of competence: historians pointed to misrepresentations of history, humanitarian workers emphasized the limits of humanitarianism, reporters reported on the tragic absurdity of treating ethnic cleansers and their victims evenhandedly, and human rights activists exposed the fallacious justifications given by Western officials for granting impunity to powerful war criminals. Once combined, however, these specific objections show that the doctrine of the international community affected the Yugoslav and Rwandan conflicts in a remarkably similar way, which can be synthesized as follows.

54

Misguiding Definitions

As already mentioned, the Yugoslav and Rwandan conflicts were defined as prototypical ethnic wars. The international community representatives contended that the peoples of the Balkans and the Great Lakes of central Africa were plagued by intractable and incendiary feelings of mutual hatred. Supposedly rooted in ancient history, fueled by a never-ending cycle of vengeance, and merely kept in check by the authoritarian states of the cold war era, these sentiments were presented as an integral part of the culture of these regions, and thus, the main cause of the sudden explosions of "ethnic" violence in the former Yugoslavia and Rwanda. Remarkably enough, this cultural explanation survived abundant and indisputable revelations that far from being the result of lawlessness and random violence, both the genocide of the Rwandan Tutsis and ethnic cleansing of what Milosevic's propaganda called "Greater Serbia" were carefully planned at the level of national governments. Although the representatives of the international community eventually recognized the responsibilities of the Serbian and Rwandan regimes, they still maintained that the ethnic cleansing campaigns launched by Milosevic in 1991 and the Rwandan genocide of 1994 were nothing but new episodes in two long histories of cultural enmity and group vengeance.

To substantiate their claim, Western officials did not hesitate to borrow their arguments from the instigators of the Yugoslav and Rwandan wars. First, they emphasized the fact that the ancestors of today's victims were once guilty of terrible crimes against the ancestors of their current victimizers. Hence, like Milosevic and his allies, Western officials traced the destruction of Vukovar in 1991 to the persecution of the Serbs by the Croatian Ustashas in the 1940s.[40] Some of them even accepted the notion that both the oppression of the Albanian Kosovars, since 1989, and the siege of Sarajevo, from 1992 to 1995, constituted some kind of payback for the battle of Kosovo in 1389, when a Serbian prince was defeated by the army of the Ottoman Empire.[41] Similarly, many Western officials, especially in France, interpreted the Rwandan genocide in the same terms as did its perpetrators. Relying on the myth—invented by the German and Belgian colonizers—that the Tutsis were a racially distinct elite who ruled Rwanda for centuries, they presented the genocide of 1994 as an act of revenge carried out by the Hutu majority against their former oppressors.[42] Second, the representatives of the international community often argued that both the Serbian onslaught and the genocide of the Tutsis started because, rightly or wrongly, the aggressors felt threatened by their future victims. They thus gave some credence to the idea that the Yugoslav army and Serbian militias intervened in Croatia and Bosnia in order to protect endangered Serbian minorities, and they also suggested that the extermination of the Rwandan Tutsis was at least partly imputable to the fact that the Hutu majority was afraid of meeting a similar fate at the hands of the Tutsi soldiers of the Rwandese Patriotic Front (RPF).[43]

When they claimed that both the Yugoslav and Rwandan wars were fueled by fears of seeing a tragic past repeat itself, the representatives of the international community did not mean to defend the instigators of these conflicts. Nonetheless, what likened their assertion to the rhetoric of the ethnic cleansers was that they referred to the use of painful memories and threatening prospects as proof of deeply ingrained popular sentiments rather than a technique of political propaganda aimed at preparing a population for war. They thus implied that genocide and systematic ethnic cleansing were the expression of an unfortunate cultural heritage of resentment and fear rather than the enactment of a precise political program by a specific political regime. It is certainly true that such a regime could not impose itself if hostile representations of its future victims were not already a part of its own people's culture; and it is also true that a vengeful and paranoid campaign has a better chance of being successful when hostile feelings and images—as well as tragic memories—exist on all sides. Yet, whatever the abrasive potential between neighboring or intertwined communities, it necessarily takes a political regime to turn latent hostility into a project, whether the latter is the physical elimination of a people or the ethnic cleansing of a territory.

In the former Yugoslavia, the main cause of the successive conflicts was the political regime instituted by Milosevic. The emergence of the Serbian leader can be traced to the crisis of the Yugoslav federation in the mid-1980s. At that time, the ruling Communist Party had to confront the same problems as most of its Central and Eastern European counterparts— namely, a deteriorating economy and a population aspiring to more political freedom. Since socialism had largely lost its credibility, some segments of the establishment realized that they needed to switch ideology, or at least rhetoric, if they wanted to remain in power. While a few officials attempted to refashion themselves as social democrats, more successful were their colleagues who substituted a nationalist agenda for Tito's ideal of socialist brotherhood between the peoples of Yugoslavia.[44]

In a multinational state made up of six republics and six "constitutive" nations, the political exaltation of national cultures—but also of chauvinistic pride and historical antagonisms—proved popular for three main reasons. First of all, it was forbidden under the Communist regime and could thus be associated with the return of free speech. Moreover, nationalism evoked such heroic feats as the resistance against the Ottoman and Austrian Empires, whereas democracy lacked a glorious record—since the resistance to Nazism had been claimed by socialism. Finally, the economic crisis was enhancing tensions between the various Yugoslav republics, especially regarding the distribution of federal funds.

Nationalism, however, did not have the same implications for all the Yugoslav republics. For Croatia and Slovenia, and later for Macedonia and Bosnia-Hercegovina, a nationalist agenda meant either demanding more autonomy—moving from a federal toward a confederate association of states—or even seeking complete independence. For Serbia, on the other hand, a nationalist agenda was not primarily associated with secession but dominance. It meant reclaiming the supremacy that Serbia had enjoyed between the two world wars —in the "first Yugoslavia" of King Alexander—but had lost under the authoritarian yet carefully balanced system instituted by Tito. Therefore, the clash of nationalisms that led to the breakup of Yugoslavia initially opposed the advocates of a loose confederation of sovereign states and the proponents of a centralized Yugoslavia dominated by Serbia.

The main instigator of the latter project was Milosevic, who seized the leadership of the Serbian Communists' League in 1987. To enlist the support of the Serbian population, Milosevic proclaimed that the separatist proclivities of the other nations were a deadly threat to the Serbs living outside of Serbia.[45] The prospect of Croatia and Bosnia's independence, as well as Kosovo's expanded sovereignty, certainly raised a legitimate concern regarding the status of the Serbian minority. What Milosevic demanded, however, was not that the future confederation protect the rights of the Serbian diaspora; rather, he argued that Serbs would never be safe if they were to live in states where they would be treated as a minority. Therefore, the Serbian leader vowed to preserve the territorial integrity of Yugoslavia, but also to increase Serbian control over the federal government.

In 1989, Milosevic suspended the autonomous governments of Vojvodina and Kosovo, thereby translating his commitments into an institutional reality.[46] Yet, both his political maneuvering and his treatment of the Kosovars after 1989 radicalized the secessionist movements in the other Yugoslav republics.[47] Therefore, by the end of 1990, Milosevic's regime gradually took another course. When it became clear to him that he could not prevent Slovenia and Croatia from becoming independent, the Serbian leader dropped his plans for a united Yugoslavia dominated by Serbia. Instead, he embraced the cause of Greater Serbia. Whereas his initial purpose had been to bring Yugoslavia under Serbian control, his new project was to gather all Serbs into one country. To this end, he set a political agenda consisting of two basic rules, which were to be implemented by all means necessary. The first rule stated that Serbia was everywhere Serbs lived; the second, that only Serbs could and should live in Serbia. The consequences of this change of regime were twofold. On the one hand, Milosevic no longer opposed the secession of Slovenia and Macedonia because the populations of these two republics did not include a substantial Serbian minority. On the other hand, the Serbian leader and his subcontractors—in Knin and Pale—launched the slaughter and deportation campaigns that purported to create Greater Serbia by cleansing a fourth of Croatia and two-thirds of Bosnia of their non-Serbian population.

In Rwanda, a political regime—that is, the regime that ruled the country between 1990 and 1994—is also to blame for the killing of about 800,000 Tutsis and antiracist Hutus. Although the actual genocide took place in the three months following the assassination of President Habyarimana, the officials who planned the extermination of the Rwandan Tutsis and the Hutus opposing their plan already imposed their agenda during the last years of Habyarimana's rule. Habyarimana himself had come to power thanks to a coup in 1973. He instituted the so-called second republic, in which his own movement, the MRND (Mouvement Républicain National pour le Développement), replaced the Hutu Party (Parmehutu) as the only legal party.[48] Though more moderate than its predecessor, the Rwandan second republic remained a despotic and structurally racist regime. Not only did Habyarimana ignore the issue of the Tutsi exiles—he claimed that the country was too small to integrate them—but he also established a system of quotas according to which public schools and national administrations were not allowed to hire more than 10 percent Tutsis. Moreover, to facilitate the implementation of this policy, passports and other identification documents had to mention the "ethnicity" of their carriers.[49]

By the end of the 1980s, the Rwandan regime suddenly came under attack, both politically and militarily. On the political front, Habyarimana's predicament resulted from the ideological turmoil that accompanied the end of the cold war. Western governments, who had supported anticommunist dictators for about forty years, now declared their intention to foster democracy in Africa. In particular, in 1990, President François Mitterrand delivered a famous speech in La Baule in which he warned "Francophone" African leaders that French aid would now be incumbent on the democratic record of its recipients. Mitterrand's pledge was largely meant to be rhetorical.[50] Still, in the wake of the La Baule announcement, some old African dictators such as Habyarimana were confronted with an emboldened opposition and eventually pressured into promising reforms.[51]

On the military front, Habyarimana had to face the consequences of his persistent refusal to even discuss the return of the Tutsi diaspora. The exiles were now represented by the RPF, a political and military organization based in Uganda, and well armed by the Ugandan government.[52] The declared objective of the RPF was to bring the exiles back to Rwanda, either through a peaceful settlement or by force. Although Habyarimana became aware of the danger, and thus addressed the issue of the refugees in 1988, the RPF did not wait for the outcome of the negotiations: in October 1990, its troops launched a major offensive from the Ugandan border.

With the help of French paratroopers, the Rwandan army managed to contain the RPF's attack and the Rwandan president remained in power. From October 1990 to April 1994, however, Habyarimana's regime changed in an apparently ambivalent but ultimately frightful way. On the one hand, the French president persuaded his Rwandan counterpart to accept the new political and military situation. Habyarimana was thus pressured into negotiating with the RPF and instituting a multiparty system. This process led to the 1993 Arusha agreements. These accords not only proclaimed Rwanda's commitment to move from autocracy to democracy; they also called for the return of the exiles and the formation of a transitional government that was to include members of the RPF.

On the other hand, Habyarimana and his entourage actively worked at undermining the reconciliation process.[53] Taking full advantage of the support granted by his French protectors, the Rwandan president sponsored the so-called Hutu Power networks, whose missions consisted of demonizing the RPF and scapegoating the Tutsi minority.[54] Accused of being the rebels' accomplices, the Tutsis, who represented about 15 percent of the Rwandan population, became both the object of murderous propaganda and the target of paramilitary death squads.[55] In short, while Habyarimana himself pretended to go along with the transitional process leading to peace and democracy, his militant entourage was developing quite a different political agenda. In order to avoid any power sharing with the RPF, their plan was simply to apply a "final solution" to the Tutsi problem. Therefore, when Habyarimana's assassination, on April 6, 1994, enabled the leaders of the Hutu Power networks to form an interim government, the new rulers decided that the time had come to carry out their grand project.[56]

There are at least three major reasons to incriminate the regimes of Milosevic and Habyarimana's entourage for the horrors of the Yugoslav and Rwandan conflicts. First, these regimes defined, respectively, the ethnic cleansing of Greater Serbia and genocide of the Tutsis as their political objectives. In addition, they resorted to relentless, murderous propaganda aimed at preparing their Serbian and Hutu constituencies for the realization of their project. Indeed, during the months preceding the beginning of the massacres, official and semiofficial media gradually raised the level of popular paranoia in order to persuade Serbs and Hutus that killing their Muslim, Croat, and Tutsi neighbors—as well as the Serbian and Hutu traitors to the patriotic cause—was nothing but a mandatory act of preventive self-defense.

Third, the Serbian and Rwandan regimes delegated the

bulk of the massacres of civilians to paramilitary death squads that were specially armed and trained for that task. The division of labor between regular armed forces and militias served two purposes. On the one hand, and especially during the early phases of the wars, it enabled the Yugoslav and Rwandan regimes to meet their objectives while maintaining legitimacy. Thanks to the militias, they could deflect mounting international outrage by blaming the extreme violence on mysterious rogue and uncontrolled elements.[57] On the other hand, assigning the rapes and massacres of civilians to other civilians enabled the Serbian and Rwandan regimes to involve large segments of the population in their criminal project.

Determined to create irreparable hostility between formerly intertwined communities, the proponents of Greater Serbia and Hutu Power even advised their militia leaders to privilege rapes and murders between acquaintances. In other words, squad members were asked, and often forced at gunpoint by their superiors, to rape and kill people from their own villages and neighborhoods.

As their use of propaganda and paramilitary militias demonstrated, the proponents of Greater Serbia and Hutu Power not only planned to gather their respective communities in an "ethnically pure" state. They also endeavored to implement their political project by drawing the Yugoslav and Rwandan societies into an ethnic war. Therefore, by interpreting the Yugoslav wars and Rwandan genocide in ethno-cultural terms, Western governments simply played into the hands of the instigators of these tragic conflicts. For if the international community had incriminated the political regimes of Habyarimana and Milosevic—instead of pontificating about the intractable bad blood between ethnic groups—it would have offered the Serbian and Rwandan Hutu societies a chance to disassociate themselves from their leaders. It might have also dissuaded the Croat, Bosnian, and RPF leaderships from embracing their own brand of sectarian nationalism.

Indeed, denouncing the political agendas of the proponents of Greater Serbia and Hutu Power does not amount to either condemning "the Serbs" and "the Hutus," or even supporting "the Croats," "the Bosnian Muslims," and "the Tutsis." To the contrary, substituting a political for a cultural analysis is the only way of truly discarding the appalling notion of collective responsibility. In other words, holding political regimes accountable for ethnic cleansing and genocide serves two major purposes: it encourages the constituents of these governments to reject the policies carried out in their name, and it deters the victims from emulating their aggressors.

Self-Serving Motives

Since the advocates of Greater Serbia and Hutu Power made so little mystery of their plans, why did Western governments downplay the responsibility of Milosevic and Habyarimana's political regimes, respectively, in the Yugoslav and Rwandan conflicts? The early reports of massive human rights violations in the former Yugoslavia and Rwanda inspired two major feelings among the leading members of the international community: a strong reluctance to intervene forcefully, and an equally powerful desire to conceal their pusillanimity. Hence their unanimous decision to favor a cultural interpretation over political analysis of the mounting violence; for the latter might have led to a military intervention against the proponents of Greater Serbia and Hutu Power, whereas the former enabled the international community to blame the intractable hatred between the various warring parties for its own inaction.

At the outset of both the Yugoslav and Rwandan crises, all
the leading members of the international community were
reluctant to act decisively, but not necessarily for the same
reasons. Some Western powers were merely concerned with
avoiding a hazardous involvement for their armed forces. This
was especially the case with the United States, despite the
fact that Clinton, as a presidential candidate, had strongly
criticized the neutrality of the Bush administration in the
early stages of the Bosnian War.[58] Once elected, however, the
president rapidly reneged on his promises to enforce international law and come to the rescue of the Bosnian people.
Constrained by the Somalian fiasco—and by his own "draft-
dodging" past—Clinton bowed to his successive joint chiefs
of staff, who did not regard systematic rapes, deportations,
and mass killings of foreign civilians as a sufficient motive to
risk the lives of U.S. soldiers.

In its new post–cold war incarnation, the U.S. military was
prepared to fight the so-called new Hitlers who were threatening the vital interests of the United States. Yet its leadership was certainly not willing to get caught in another "Vietnam quagmire"—especially after U.S. marines were killed in
Somalia—for the sake of the international community and
its commitments to human rights and democracy. Therefore,
during the first years of Clinton's presidency, foreign policy
amounted to an uneasy compromise between the ambitions
of an administration eager to appear as the benign but reso-
lute leader of the new international community and the tight
restrictions that the Pentagon imposed on these ambitions.

Regarding the former Yugoslavia, until the summer of
1995, Clinton's cabinet often seemed split between the advocates of the Pentagon, who insisted that nonintervention remain the bedrock of U.S. diplomacy, and those foreign policy
advisers who tried to maintain the moral high ground that
had characterized the 1992 campaign.[59] Despite the efforts of

some State Department officials, however, the overt and obstinate refusal of the U.S. military to send in ground troops compelled the administration to endorse the strategy of appeasement favored by its European allies.

As for Rwanda, in spite of the fact that Ugandan President Yoweri Museveni—at the time, the RPF's protector—was the main protégé of the United States in central Africa, the Somalian precedent acted as a particularly strong deterrent against any type of U.S. intervention. The Clinton administration thus deployed unequaled efforts to avoid the involvement of U.S. troops. Indeed, from April to June 1994, representatives of the U.S. government were explicitly instructed not to use the word *genocide* to describe the extermination of the Tutsis and the moderate Hutus because, according to the 1948 Convention for the Prevention of Genocides, it would have forced the United States to take part in a military intervention under the UN flag.[60]

While Clinton's main concern was to comply with the demands of his military establishment, some European leaders had different motives for refusing to single out the promoters of Greater Serbia and Hutu Power as the instigators of the wars. In particular, Mitterrand displayed a persistent indulgence for Milosevic's regime and supported the rule of Habyarimana, and his successors, to the bitter end.[61] Haunted by memories of World War I—that is, the old alliance between Paris, London, Belgrade, and Moscow against Berlin, Vienna, and Zagreb—the aging French president saw a dominant and Francophile Serbia as the best way of both maintaining stability in the Balkans and balancing German influence in Central Europe. Therefore, taking advantage of the fact that none of his European and U.S. allies had much stomach for a forceful intervention, Mitterrand became the main exponent of a nonpartisan diplomacy that was objectively favoring Serbia, since the latter had the military upper hand. In other words, while emphatically deploring the ills of nationalism, the French president nonetheless invited his partners in the international community to accept the consequences of the ethnic cleansing campaigns as a regrettable fait accompli.[62]

As far as Rwanda was concerned, it is true that Mitterrand pressured Habyarimana into signing the 1993 Arusha agreements, which were designed to establish a pluralist democracy, organize the return of the Tutsi exiles, and integrate the RPF into the new political landscape. Yet the French president also saw three good reasons to protect his Rwandan counterpart at all costs.[63] First, Habyarimana was an old protégé of France. By defending him, then, Mitterrand was conveying to all the other francophone dictators of Africa that in spite of France's new stance on development and democracy, he would not let them down. Second, the very prospect of Rwanda's imminent democratization enhanced Mitterrand's support of Habyarimana. Convinced that, in Africa, ethnicity means more than ideology, Mitterrand thought it wise to favor the man who portrayed himself as the champion of the Hutu majority. Third, and most important, the privileged status of Habyarimana was motivated by Mitterrand's perception that the Rwandan Hutus were Francophone, and thus Francophile, while the Tutsi exiles were not only Anglophone but also — along with their Ugandan allies — agents of the growing influence of the United States in central Africa.[64]

Each for his own political reasons, both the U.S. and French presidents refrained from pointing too strongly at the regimes of Milosevic and Habyarimana, respectively, for the ethnic cleansing campaigns in Croatia and Bosnia and the mounting violence in Rwanda.[65] Because U.S. vital interests were not at stake, the main concern of the Clinton administration was to display the moral and political leadership of the United States at the lowest possible cost, in human as well as financial terms. As such, the U.S. government refrained from granting the new Hitler status to the proponents of Greater Serbia and Hutu Power because such a characterization would have forced the United States to meet its post–Gulf War responsibilities. Instead, the administration grudgingly embraced the ethno-cultural definition of both the Yugoslav and Rwandan disputes. Although this did not necessarily reflect the views of the entire cabinet, it had the decisive advantage of justifying the Pentagon's refusal to risk the lives of U.S. soldiers.

As for the French authorities, their primary concern was to ward off France's decline in the post–cold war world, both by challenging Germany's hegemony in Central Europe and by curtailing the rising influence of the United States in central Africa. Since French officials saw the Croats, Bosnian Muslims, and Tutsis as the allies of their Western rivals, they urged the international community to take an "impartial" approach to both the Yugoslav and Rwandan conflicts — namely, one that would not endeavor to deprive the proponents of Greater Serbia and Hutu Power of their dominant positions. More than any other Western government, France thus claimed that ancient hatreds, rather than the political agendas of Milosevic and Habyarimana, were the main cause of the violence in the former Yugoslavia and Rwanda.

Remarkably, despite their divergent interests and motivations, the leading members of the international community succeeded in keeping a largely united front during the Yugoslav and Rwandan crises. From a tactical point of view, it is certainly true that they often blamed each other for the less than glorious results of their collective efforts. France, for instance, repeatedly accused Germany of favoring Croatia, and chastised the United States both for giving false hopes to the Bosnian Muslims and secretly supporting the RPF rebellion. Meanwhile, the United States criticized France, Britain, and Russia for their pro-Serbian bias, and incriminated French neocolonial practices for the crisis in Rwanda. The

U.S. government also defended its relative passivity in the former Yugoslavia by claiming that it was primarily a European responsibility, whereas European countries denounced the United States for holding a moralistic position but refusing to pay any price for it. Finally, both the United States and its European allies stigmatized the incompetence and paralysis of the UN bureaucracy, while UN officials reproached the member states for their lack of military and financial support. Yet, despite their multiple quarrels, Western governments and international institutions agreed to invoke the ethno-cultural nature of the Yugoslav and Rwandan conflicts in order to justify their own limited involvement.[66] The failures of the international community, then, should not be attributed to the lack of cohesion among its leading members but to the consistent strategy that Western governments managed to devise.

Obfuscating Policies

The successive policies that Western governments and international institutions applied to the wars in the former Yugoslavia and Rwanda were not just predicated on the premise that the two conflicts were about age-old ethnic hatreds. The implementation of these policies actually purported to demonstrate the accuracy of this assumption, and thus, ward off a political understanding of both the Yugoslav and Rwandan crises. To begin with, during the wars, one of the main tasks of the peacekeepers and mediators mandated by the international community was to convey that there was no viable alternative to humanitarian and diplomatic efforts. As well, even in the aftermath of the Dayton Peace Agreements and the RPF's takeover of Kigali, the reconstruction and reconciliation policies initiated by the international community failed to revise, or at least draw proper lessons from, the ethno-cultural definitions initially projected onto the two conflicts.

Humanitarianism

The humanitarian missions conducted under the UN umbrella —UNPROFOR in the former Yugoslavia and operation "Turquoise" in Rwanda—went through different phases. At first, the mandates defined by the Security Council were hailed as the appropriate response to the ethnically motivated civil wars that were allegedly plaguing the former Yugoslavia and Rwanda. As already mentioned, these mandates implied that in order to accomplish their humanitarian tasks—namely, providing food and medical assistance to civilian populations —the peacekeepers were to remain impartial. They were thus requested to avoid confrontation with the warring parties, unless they were deliberately targeted.

In time, however, the reports of humanitarian agencies, human rights groups, and war correspondents gave the Western public a clearer picture of what was actually going on in the former Yugoslavia and Rwanda. A growing number of people began emphasizing that neutrality in the face of ethnic cleansing and genocide amounted to a passive complicity with the perpetrators of these crimes. Consequently, the leading members of the international community experienced increasing difficulties justifying the neutrality of the peacekeepers operating in their name. Worried about a possible outcry of their public opinions, Western governments eventually modified their stance: instead of defending the validity of their humanitarian option, they simply stated that because it was now in motion, the peacekeeping efforts prevented them from changing course. In other words, the representatives of the international community argued that while a partisan and forceful intervention was maybe not unjustified, either the safety of the peacekeepers on the ground — in Bosnia — or the completion of their humanitarian mission — in Rwanda — still made it impossible.

In the former Yugoslavia, the soldiers operating under UNPROFOR were initially assigned two tasks: they were to curb the violence both by taking up positions on the frontlines and taking possession of the heavy weapons that were in their zones of operation; and they were to ensure the safe passage of humanitarian aid to the civilian population caught in the fighting. Although these missions served the immediate purposes of Western governments — displaying their concern for civilian victims without entering the war — they also forced the peacekeepers into an objective alliance with the Serbian militias.

To convey that they had no intention of entering the fighting, UN troops were both lightly armed and deliberately deployed in vulnerable positions. In particular, the battalions that were supposed to protect the so-called safe areas — the Bosnian cities of Sarajevo, Tuzla, Gorazde, Srebrenica, Zepa, and Bihac — had no way of imposing their authority on the Bosnian Serb militias that were besieging these cities. Indeed, contrary to UNPROFOR and the incipient Bosnian army, whose development was seriously hindered by the UN arms embargo on all "parties" to the war, the Serbian forces were actively assisted and generously equipped by the Yugoslav army. Not only were the peacekeepers incapable of opposing the shelling of besieged cities and ongoing practice of ethnic cleansing but they could not even fulfill their humanitarian missions without the permission of the Bosnian Serb leaders, Radovan Karadzic and Ratko Mladic.

Practically, the Bosnian Serb leadership allowed UN blue helmets to deliver humanitarian aid to Bosnian civilians under three conditions: UNPROFOR had to give a substantial share of the international aid to the Bosnian Serb warlords; in spite of their mandate, UN troops had to let the Bosnian Serb militias keep their heavy weapons; and UNPROFOR's spokespeople had to refrain from blaming the war on the Serbian side alone. The Serbian leadership, in other words, collaborated with the peacekeepers on the condition that the UN remain faithful to the ethno-cultural definition of the war, regardless of the peacekeepers' experience on the ground. As a result, from 1992 to 1994, the successive UN commanders consistently shielded the Serbian militias by condemning "all sides" for resorting to violence.

In the early months of 1994, however, justifying UNPROFOR's "neutrality" became an increasingly challenging task for the representatives of the international community: the horrendous images of Sarajevo's market after the shelling of February 5, the Serbian offensive against the UN safe area of Gorazde in April, but also the end of the war between Bosnian Croats and Bosnian Muslims—at the end of March—made it almost impossible not to single out the Bosnian Serb militias as both the cause of the ongoing war and main perpetrators of atrocities. Nervous about the reactions of their own constituents, Western governments could no longer contend that the ethno-cultural nature of the conflict demanded that they remain neutral and limit their intervention to humanitarian efforts.[67] Therefore, rather than defending the principles governing their policy, the leading members of the international community simply decided to flaunt what they called their powerlessness. They maintained that they could neither risk a NATO intervention—whether on the ground or from the air—nor even lift the arms embargo unilaterally in favor of the Bosnian army because such moves would endanger the lives of the UNPROFOR peacekeepers.

In Rwanda, the mostly French—yet UN sponsored—intervention known as operation Turquoise was launched at the end of June 1994. Although other leading members of the international community questioned the motives of the French authorities, the Security Council had no choice but to authorize the operation because of its own shameful attitude in the first days of the genocide. Indeed, on April 21, 1994, two weeks after the beginning of the massacres, the Security Council had simply decided to withdraw most of the 2,500 blue helmets that had been sent the year before, in order to supervise the implementation of the Arusha agreements.

Like the UNPROFOR peacekeepers in the former Yugoslavia, the French soldiers involved in operation Turquoise were sent as a neutral force invested with a humanitarian mission.[68] According to the Security Council's resolution authorizing their
intervention, French troops did not come to Rwanda either to stop the genocide of the Tutsis or even to rescue the survivors of the massacres perpetrated by the Rwandan Armed Forces and Hutu militias. Their mandate stipulated that they were to remain impartial and neutral, and use all means necessary in order to provide food and medical assistance to the unspecified victims of a humanitarian crisis. Since France had been known to support Habyarimana's regime, Mitterrand was particularly proud to announce that while his country was the only one to do something about the Rwandan situation, French troops were not going to side with any of the "warring factions"; they would simply try to save the lives of civilians, regardless of their ethnicity.

By the time Turquoise was operational, however, both the genocide of the Tutsis and military defeat of their murderers were already faits accomplis. In keeping with their humanitarian mandate, French troops were primarily assigned to protect the exodus of about two million Hutus, who under the guidance of the Rwandan Armed Forces and Interahamwe militias, were fleeing from advancing RPF troops. Hence the enthusiastic reception of Turquoise among Hutu militias, while the RPF saw the French operation as a hostile intervention. The French peacekeepers managed to establish a "security zone" covering about one-fifth of Rwanda's territory and a portion of the Kivu province, in the former Zaire. In that area, Turquoise's record can be summarized as follows: on the one hand, French troops imposed a cease-fire, provided humanitarian relief to the Hutu population on their way to Zaire, and saved the lives of about 10,000 Tutsi refugees from the city of Cyangugu; on the other hand, they offered shelter and a safe escape to the officers, politicians, and militia leaders who organized the genocide.[69]

Barely a few weeks into the French intervention, the mandate of operation Turquoise had become indefensible. First, on July 1, 1994, the Security Council at last recognized that the humanitarian crisis in Rwanda was probably a genocide. Then, on July 17, the RPF claimed a complete victory and declared the war's end. Two days later, a government of national unity took office in Kigali and was immediately recognized by the international community. Finally, on July 28, the UN secretary general ordered an investigation of what was now officially called a genocide.

Meanwhile, however, French troops were still protecting the executioners of the massacres: not only did they fail to arrest them but, faithful to their impartial stance, they denied access to the security zone to the new Rwandan authorities. To justify its position, the French government could no longer rely on the notion that the Interahamwe militias and former rebels of the RPF were two ethnic factions that just needed to be separated. In order to spare their former protégés, French officials argued that their humanitarian mission required them to provide relief to a suffering population—especially since a cholera epidemic had broken out in the security zone—rather than engage in police activities that were not included in their mandate. In short, even when the international community finally recognized that the Rwandan crisis should not have called for an impartial humanitarian intervention, such a mission could still be used to defuse political responsibilities.

Diplomacy

The diplomatic efforts deployed by the international community in the former Yugoslavia and Rwanda call for the same kind of judgment as their humanitarian endeavors. In both cases, the representatives of the international community obfuscated the nature of the conflicts in order to minimize the cost of their own involvement. Regarding the international community's attempts at mediating the Yugoslav and Rwandan disputes, their unfortunate evolution can be described as follows.

At the very outset of the two crises, the leading members of the international community already positioned themselves as mediators. Yet the principles that they forwarded were still in conformity with their professed values: the Rwandan peace process launched in 1990 called for democratic reforms and the return of the Tutsi exiles, while the 1991 conference on Yugoslavia ruled that the Yugoslav republics had the right to secede — provided that the constitutions of the new states protected the rights of minorities — and international borders could not be modified by force.[70] Nevertheless, when Habyarimana and Milosevic's regimes obviously and ruthlessly transgressed these principles, the international community refused to assume its responsibilities.

In Rwanda, neither the "rehearsal" massacres perpetrated by the proponents of Hutu Power nor even the clear warning, sent by UN Commander Roméo Dallaire, that a genocide was imminent managed to persuade international institutions and Western governments that their commitment to the Arusha process required them to take action against the party that was blatantly betraying it.[71] Similarly, in the former

Yugoslavia, neither the military occupation of a fourth of Croatia nor the explicit threat delivered by Karadzic succeeded in convincing the sponsors of the conference on Yugoslavia that they had an obligation to enforce their own rulings.[72]

Instead of defending the principles that they had delineated, and thus forcing Habyarimana and Milosevic to abide by them, the leading members of the international community endeavored to preserve their position of neutral mediators, regardless of the evolution of the conflicts. Claiming that their primary objective was to promote peace, they maintained that a negotiated settlement between the warring factions was the only way to end the violence. In order to retain their capacity to mediate the negotiations, they argued, they could simply not afford to appear too hostile to one of the parties.

In Rwanda, the sponsors of the Arusha agreements persistently turned a blind eye to the nature of the mounting horror: not only did UNAMIR leave the country almost as soon as the genocide began but, five weeks later, the UN was still pursuing its mediating efforts.[73] Indeed, on May 17, 1994, the Security Council responded to the slaughter of several hundred thousand civilians by asking for a cease-fire between their killers and the RPF. Although this call for a truce—and even a negotiated settlement—between the so-called warring factions amounted to a deliberate denial of the genocide, it remained the official position of the Security Council until July 1. Therefore, when the Turquoise peacekeepers arrived in Rwanda, in the last weeks of June, the French authorities tried to exploit the pusillanimity of their Western partners in order to prevent the RPF from taking over the entire country. Claiming that, as representatives of the international community, they were to act as neutral mediators, French officials pleaded once again for a cease-fire and settlement that would include the interim government and Rwandan Armed Forces.

While the complete victory of the RPF put a rapid end to the French "mediation" in Rwanda, in the former Yugoslavia, the international community held on to its neutral stance for about four years. The policy developed jointly by the French president, British prime minister, and secretary general of the UN was based on the idea that the representatives of the international community should be exemplary: rather than imitating the brutal ways of the local warring factions, they were to take the high ground and teach the peoples of the former Yugoslavia to choose dialogue over violence. Practically speaking, this lofty approach meant that each time Milosevic and his Bosnian Serb henchmen would refuse to comply with Security Council resolutions, instead of resorting to violence, the international community would ask its seasoned diplomats to accommodate the Serbian authorities by modifying the terms of the ongoing dialogue.

Since their employers were not prepared to oppose Serbian aggression—either by intervening militarily or by allowing the Croats and Bosnians to defend themselves—the special envoys of the international community were to act as if there was no aggression to repel. In Bosnia especially, their assignment was to portray the conflict in a way that justified both their own neutrality and the contention of the international community that a negotiated settlement precluded the use of force against one of the parties. The Bosnian Serb leaders, then, were never coerced into either signing the Vance-Owen and Contact Group peace plans or withdrawing their troops from the surroundings of the besieged safe areas. Instead, the special envoys of the international community consistently demanded that "all sides" sacrifice at least part of their "nationalist" agenda in the name of peace. Such evenhandedness implied that the Bosnian authorities were pressured into recognizing their military defeat, while Karadzic and Mladic were begged to settle for a partial victory.

Although well designed to preserve the neutrality of the international community, the diplomatic approach advocated by Mitterrand, Major, and Boutros-Ghali was eventually bound to fail. First, emboldened by the passivity of the international community, the Bosnian Serb leaders saw no reason to compromise. They were determined to reject all peace plans that would offer them less than a completely cleansed and fully integrated Greater Serbia. Furthermore, impressed by the acquiescence of the international community to the Serbian conquests, Croatian President Franjo Tudjman was increasingly tempted to absorb an ethnically cleansed Herceg-Bosna—that is, the southwestern region of Bosnia—into a "Greater Croatia." Third, fully aware of their impending fate, the Bosnian authorities could not agree to a capitulation that would have amounted to collective suicide.

Given all this, in the summer of 1995, the representatives of the international community realized that they only had two options left: they could either withdraw their peacekeepers, drop their diplomatic efforts, and accept the carving up of Bosnia between a Greater Serbia and a Greater Croatia, or they could revise their contention that a negotiated settlement precluded the use of force. Concerned about the reaction of their public opinions if they chose the first option—especially after the Rwandan genocide of 1994, the humiliation of the UNPROFOR blue helmets by Mladic's troops in May 1995, and the tragic fall of Srebrenica, a UN safe area, in July 1995—Western governments finally decided to confront Milosevic's followers.

Reconstruction

In retrospect, the representatives of the international community recognized that a genocide had taken place in Rwanda —thereby admitting that they did not meet their obligation to prevent it—and a military intervention would have been necessary to end the war in the former Yugoslavia. Although these tardy and often muddled acknowledgments constituted an implicit condemnation of the humanitarian and diplomatic policies pursued by the international community during the two conflicts, Western governments neither formally repudiated their previous approach nor even questioned the ethnocultural premise on which their policies were predicated—at least until the sudden crisis of their doctrine in the spring of 1999.

The leading members of the international community avoided revising—or even reviewing—their initial assessment of the Rwandan and Yugoslav situations because such a revision would have both incriminated them for their past conduct and set an excessively challenging precedent for their future decisions. Indeed, if Western officials had publicly recognized that the ethnic cleansing campaigns and genocide should have been attributed to overt political projects, rather than ingrained cultural enmities, they might have exposed themselves to embarrassing questions and exaggerated expectations.

On the one hand, as leading members of the international community, Western officials could have been required to explain why they had let the Serbian and Rwandan regimes successively express their ideals of racial purity, deploy their propaganda machines, and train their death squads without ever exposing them as the deadly menaces that they represented. Answering such questions would have been all the more embarrassing because the end of the cold war was supposed to revive the hopes and ideals that accompanied the end of World War II, and especially, the allies' solemn vow that genocidal regimes would "never again" be tolerated. On the other hand, Western leaders could also have been asked to draw lessons from their past failures, and thus be expected to amend their doctrine for future purposes. In other words, by focusing too much on the responsibilities of Habyarimana and Milosevic's regimes, the representatives of the international community would have been prevented from using the ancient hatred alibi again, either to limit their involvement in the political reconstruction of Rwanda and former Yugoslavia or to justify their inaction in similar crises elsewhere.

Because minimizing the reassessment of their doctrine served the interests of Western governments, the political dimensions of post–cold war conflicts continued to be obfuscated, even in the aftermath of the Bosnian and Rwandan wars. While the international community's representatives proclaimed their determination to help Bosnia and Rwanda move from civil war to democracy, the transitional processes that they supported were still about transcending age-old ethnic hatreds. More precisely, they endeavored to associate Bosnia and Rwanda's transitions to democracy with the reconciliation of antagonized ethnic groups rather than the stigmatization of the political regimes that had advocated ethnic cleansing. In accordance with this approach, the local leaders with whom the international community negotiated its involvement in the reconstruction of Bosnia and Rwanda were not perceived in terms of their ideological persuasion and political agenda but merely treated as the representatives of their respective ethnic communities.

In the former Yugoslavia, between spring 1994 and summer 1995, the international community gradually moved away from its strictly humanitarian and neutral stance. First, as soon as Tudjman and his protégés of Herceg-Bosna signed a peace treaty in March 1994 with the government of Sarajevo, the Clinton administration agreed to secretly provide the Bosnians and Croats with some military equipment, despite the arms embargo. Second, when Jacques Chirac succeeded Mitterrand in May 1995, the newly elected French president put an end to the self-inflicted powerlessness of

UNPROFOR by imposing the creation of the Rapid Reaction Force. Then, late that summer, the international community finally decided to take action against the Bosnian Serb militias: on August 29, one day after Mladic's troops provoked yet another massacre on Sarajevo's market, NATO planes started to bomb Serbian positions, while the Rapid Reaction Force prevented Serbian militias from retaliating against civilians and peacekeepers. A few weeks later, besieged Bosnian cities were freed, large portions of the country were reconquered by the forces of the Muslim-Croat Federation, and Milosevic agreed to a cease-fire on behalf of the Bosnian Serbs; in short, the war was over.

Yet, in spite of the spectacular success of their new strategy — or maybe because of it — the leading members of the international community never assumed responsibility for the catastrophic effects of their previous approach. Eager to downplay the impact of NATO's intervention, many European and UN officials even contended that far from signaling a doctrinal change, the military campaign of September 1995 had merely represented a more forceful way of obtaining what they wanted all along, namely, a negotiated settlement between the warring factions. Although usually forwarded by supporters of Mitterrand, Major, or Boutros-Ghali, this assertion was largely vindicated by the framework of the Bosnian peace accord signed in Dayton, in November 1995.

The advocates of the Dayton agreements stressed that the parties to the treaty — that is, the Serbian, Croatian, and Bosnian presidents — not only recognized Bosnia-Hercegovina's sovereignty and democratic institutions but also acknowledged that refugees should be allowed to return to their prewar residences, and that indicted war criminals should be prosecuted. Therefore, the U.S. sponsors of the accord claimed that the Dayton peace would pave the way for the reconstitution of a multicultural society, and even a multiethnic polity, within the whole territory of Bosnia-Hercegovina. Both the structure of the Dayton agreements and the way in which the accords were implemented, however, have so far belied the professed objective of their sponsors.

In October 1995, the representatives of the international community pressured the advancing forces of the Muslim-Croat Federation into declaring a cease-fire, thereby depriving them of a military victory over the Bosnian Serb militias. Instead of letting the Bosnian army dismantle the self-proclaimed "Serbian Republic," as the Croatian troops had done in western Slavonia and the Krajina region, the U.S. sponsors of the Dayton agreements opted for the following process. They established an expedient, albeit unfounded, distinction between the Serbian leader, Milosevic, and his Bosnian Serb subcontractors, Karadzic and Mladic: while the latter two, who had already been indicted for war crimes, were excluded from the negotiations, the former acquired peacemaker status simply by recognizing the sovereignty of the Bosnian state, and thus became the official representative of the Bosnian Serbs.

Next, in exchange for Milosevic's "moderation," the organizers of the Dayton peace talks agreed to partially compensate the Bosnian Serbs for the loss of an ethnically pure Greater Serbia. Hence the division of Bosnia into two largely autonomous entities: an ethnically cleansed Serbian Republic, on 49 percent of the Bosnian territory, and the Muslim-Croat Federation. Yet, once Milosevic had obtained what he wanted—namely, that the results of four years of ethnic cleansing would not be overturned by the peace agreements —the U.S. mediators were in no position to dissuade his Croatian and Bosnian counterparts from emulating their enemy. Indeed, because of their concessions to the Serbian party, the sponsors of the Dayton agreements lacked the moral authority either to oppose the separatist tendencies of Tudjman's protégés in Herceg-Bosna or prevent Izetbegovic from dropping his defense of a multicultural Bosnia and returning to the Muslim nationalist stance that had been his political persuasion before the war.

Because the framework of the Dayton negotiations defined Milosevic, Tudjman, and Izetbegovic as the leaders of their respective ethnic groups—thereby putting them on an equal moral footing—it encouraged the three presidents to privilege the defense of their communities' interests. Moreover, in the aftermath of Dayton, little was done to modify the picture of Bosnia as a place dominated by conflicting nationalisms. In particular, the measures that were supposed to erode the strict division of the country along "ethnic" lines were never implemented. Arguing that the stability of Bosnia should take precedence over any other considerations, NATO troops consistently refused to arrest Karadzic and Mladic, while only a small number of refugees were allowed to go home. Consequently, the supporters of ethnic cleansing—who still held power in the Serbian Republic and Herceg-Bosna in the fall of 1999—could proudly claim that they did not kill, rape, and deport their neighbors in vain, while the ruling Muslim nationalist wing of Izetbegovic's party could deride the forlorn hopes of their compatriots who fought for a multicultural and secular Bosnia.

In Rwanda, the military victory of the RPF in July 1994 could have enticed the representatives of the international community to confront their own responsibilities and reassess their doctrine. For contrary to the former Yugoslavia, where Milosevic's lasting power was often invoked to justify the compromises of the Dayton process, Rwanda was no longer ruled by the proponents of Hutu Power. Moreover, after the fall of the Mobutu regime in ex-Zaire, most of the organizers of the genocide were not only indicted for their crimes but also arrested and transferred to the war crimes tribunal in Arusha. Nonetheless, even if Clinton and, to a lesser extent, Annan apologized for their passivity before as well as during the Rwandan genocide, on the whole, the leading members of the international community failed to either publicly assess the motives for their actions—or lack thereof—or formally repudiate the rhetoric that they used to cover up their criminal negligence.[74]

Exemplary of the longevity of this rhetoric were the conclusions of the report on France's role in Rwanda, from 1990 to 1994, commissioned in 1998 by the French National Assembly. While the authors recognized that a certain number of mistakes were made—French diplomats underestimated the authoritarian and racist nature of Habyarimana's regime, the French military worked too closely with the Rwandan Armed Forces, and French authorities failed to take concrete action to prevent the genocide—at the same time, they continued to justify the logic behind France's policy. According to the report, the decision made by the French authorities to provide military assistance to Habyarimana's army was principled because its purpose was to level the field, and thus, establish a base for fair negotiations between the weakened Hutu majority and the much stronger Tutsi forces of the RPF. As late as December 1998, in other words, the French National Assembly still envisioned the Rwandan tragedy of the early 1990s in terms of a tribal dispute between two ethnic groups.

In the aftermath of the Rwandan war—and particularly after the fall of Mobutu—the United States replaced France as the most influential Western power in the region. Under U.S. guidance, the international community adopted what could be called a dual policy vis-à-vis the new Rwandan regime. On the one hand, Western governments added insult to injury by failing to properly acknowledge what had happened between April and July 1994. Eager to minimize revelations of their past mistakes, they never offered a symbolic recognition equal to the facts that a genocide had taken place in Rwanda, that UN officials and Western governments had been warned about it, and that fifty years after the end of World War II, they had let it happen. On the other hand, and as a form of trade off for not examining its own moral and political record, the U.S. administration convinced its partners in the international community to muffle their criticism of the new Rwandan government, whether for its treatment of prisoners or the brutal crackdowns of its armed forces on Hutu civilians.[75]

While failing to help the Rwandan authorities in their attempt to come to terms with the genocide, for fear of having their own responsibilities exposed, the U.S. government started granting them the dubious privileges due to an agent of regional stability. In short, rather than facing the truth about the past, U.S. officials chose to turn a blind eye to the human rights violations committed by the new regime. Understandably, the RPF and its allies were affected by this dual policy: whereas the members of the governing coalition who were trying to found the new Rwanda on the rejection of institutionalized racism never received the material support and symbolic recognition they needed, the proponents of a Tutsi hegemony—modeled after the military dictatorship in Burundi—took full advantage of the impunity granted by the international community.[76] The former gradually lost their credibility as a result, while the latter gained control over the Rwandan government.

Justice

To complement the process of political reconstruction, the leading members of the international community also committed themselves to the pursuit of justice in the former Yugoslavia and Rwanda. Such a commitment translated into the creation of the two International War Crimes Tribunals.[77]

Taking their cue from the human rights community, Western governments based their support for the tribunals on the claim that prosecuting war crimes and crimes against humanity is a necessary step in the transitional process that is to move a society from civil war to democracy. Indeed, according to liberal theory, the fact that individuals are held accountable for their actions is not only evidence that the rule of law has replaced the reign of force and impunity but also a powerful deterrent to the attribution of collective responsibility, and thus, the perpetuation of group vengeance.

Though undeniably a positive development, the creation of the two tribunals was primarily designed to palliate the passivity of the international community. In other words, the war crimes tribunals were substitutes for, rather than complements to, forceful interventions in the Yugoslav and Rwandan conflicts. This characterization especially applies to the tribunal for the former Yugoslavia, which was established during the war, at a moment when the international community was careful to avoid taking action against the people most likely to be indicted by the new court. The irony of the situation was expressed by the fact that the Security Council instituted the war crimes tribunals as part of the peacemaking powers of the UN—via chapter 7 of the UN Charter—whereas UNPROFOR had been invested with a peacekeeping mission. Troops were thus sent to Bosnia in order to keep a nonexistent peace, while a toothless tribunal in the Netherlands was meant to end a real war.

Because the war crimes tribunals were created as a compensation rather than a sign of doctrinal change, it is hardly surprising that both the means and autonomy granted to the courts' magistrates were strictly limited. More precisely, the support that the tribunals originally received from their sponsors was constrained by two types of considerations. As already mentioned, the leading members of the international community invoked their concern with regional stability—and so, with the security of their own troops—both to justify their reluctance to arrest indicted war criminals and to dissuade the tribunals from indicting political figures who were included in the peace process.[78] In addition, Western governments made their support for the tribunals incumbent on the assurance that their own military and civilian representatives would escape the magistrates' scrutiny. In order to avoid any embarrassment, they even considered the possibility of preventing their agents from collaborating with the courts.[79] Western officials soon realized that such radical measures could easily backfire, however: by refusing to cooperate with an institution that they were allegedly supporting, the representatives of the international community would not only expose their own contradictions but also raise even more suspicion about their past actions. Therefore, instead of simply withholding information, they decided to pressure the prosecutors of the two tribunals into clearing their officers and diplomats of all suspicion before allowing them to testify.[80]

Having limited the scope of the tribunals' investigations, the representatives of the international community still owed it to their own doctrine to prevent the rulings of the new institution from underscoring the political nature of the Yugoslav and Rwandan conflicts. According to Western officials, the ultimate purpose of the International War Crimes Tribunals consisted of facilitating the process of reconciliation between the antagonized communities of Bosnia and Rwanda. As they envisioned it, however, reconciliation was a "healing process" whereby these communities would gradually renounce the resentments and prejudices that they had held against each other for centuries. Because such a process required that past violence be treated with a wise mixture of fair retribution and mutual forgiveness, the leading members of the international community argued that the essential, if not only, task of the tribunals was to substitute individual accountability for collective responsibility. In other words, they wanted the courts to help ward off what they saw as the main obstacles to reconciliation: the perpetuation of age-old ethnic hatred and the cyclic return of group vengeance. To that end, the main message that Western governments wanted the courts' rulings to convey was that crimes can never be attributed to a people—be it Serbs, Croats, Muslims, Hutus, or Tutsis—but only to the individuals who actually committed them. Any human rights activist would obviously expect a war crimes tribunal to undermine the notion of collective responsibility and uphold the principle of individual accountability. Yet, subsuming the mission of the tribunals under this distinctive opposition, as was the wish of Western governments, would have amounted to focusing the courts' attention on individual criminals at the expense of the political project that they embodied.

True to their doctrine, the representatives of the international community were equating the process leading from ethnic cleansing and genocide to national reconciliation with a cultural leap—this time, from the tribalist notion of collective responsibility to the liberal principle of individual accountability. What this equation implied was that the massive human rights violations committed by the proponents of Greater Serbia and Hutu Power were primarily the expression of a primitive mentality that needed to be overcome. Conversely, if genocide and ethnic cleansing were perceived as the implementation of two political projects, then reconciliation—either among Serbs, Croats, and Muslims or between Hutus and Tutsis—would not be a question of cultural progress. Rather, it would mainly be incumbent on the official repudiation, at the national as well as international level, of the regimes that both advocated ethnic purity and endeavored to turn their ideal into a reality. According to this latter position, the task of the International War Crimes Tribunals would be not only to prosecute particular crimes and convict their individual perpetrators but also to use these specific cases in order to stigmatize the political regimes that promoted ethnic antagonism and prescribed ethnicist violence.

While the representatives of the international community were eager to claim the legacy of the Nuremberg trials, the type of national reconciliation that they wanted the war crimes tribunals to serve was a far cry from what the allies had in mind at the end of World War II. In 1945, the issue was not to reconcile the Nazis with their enemies and victims but to make reconciliation with Germany incumbent on its rejection of Nazism. Though rapidly trumped by the cold war, the political purpose of the Nuremberg trials was to found a new international community on such a rejection. Indeed, what was on trial in Nuremberg was neither the German people nor merely a collection of war criminals and criminals against humanity: first and foremost, it was the Nazi regime itself, through a selection of individuals who implemented its mode of government. Now it is true that a political regime is not a legal subject, which means that, technically, it cannot be tried. Yet, the Nuremberg trials were useful precisely because they succeeded in circumventing this difficulty. While they only sentenced individuals, and thus avoided the unacceptable notion of collective responsibility, the Nuremberg magistrates nevertheless purported and managed to stigmatize the Nazi regime. Likewise, if the tribunals in The Hague and Arusha were to follow the path established in 1945, they would neither condemn "the Serbs" and "the Hutus" nor merely sentence individual criminals, but by means of the latter, denounce the political regimes that called for ethnic cleansing and genocide.

In the post–cold war era, some societies did succeed in incorporating the Nuremberg rationale into their transition to democracy. In countries such as South Africa or the Czech

Republic, for instance, the new authorities did not simply expose the abuses committed by their predecessors. More important, they based their call for national reconciliation on an emphatic denunciation of the very nature of the previous regimes. In South Africa, especially, the fact that apartheid itself was branded as a crime against humanity—a qualification supported by a resolution of the UN General Assembly—was key in the reconciliation process promoted by Nelson Mandela. Rather than just relying on individual punishment and collective forgiveness, the South African president was careful to frame his call for reconciliation in political terms.

That South African authorities gave priority to politics did not mean that they compromised legal and moral principles. Indeed, tracing the crimes perpetrated by the agents of apartheid to the criminal nature of the regime itself neither exonerated the individuals who committed these crimes nor incriminated "whites" as the group that benefited from them. But while they avoided holding the white minority collectively responsible for the crimes of apartheid, the new authorities stressed that reconciliation had to be based on the stigmatization of a political system, not merely the prosecution of a discrete number of reprehensible acts. Remarkably, this emphasis on exposing apartheid as a repugnant regime was also what enabled the South African Truth and Reconciliation Commission to pardon criminals who agreed to testify. According to the commission, having executioners of the old racist rule publicly reveal the shameful truth about their former activities was the most efficient way to found reconciliation on the rejection of apartheid. The commission's argument for granting amnesty was not that reconciliation should take precedence over justice but that the public exposure of a criminal system would serve to strengthen democracy even better than a criminal sentence.

Contrary to how the allies at the end of World War II and

the new democratic authorities in South Africa, respectively, dealt with Nazism and apartheid, the representatives of the international community were intent on downplaying the part of Hutu Power in the Rwandan genocide and Greater Serbia in the Yugoslav wars. Hence, they did not wish to pattern the war crimes tribunals after either the Nuremberg courts or the South African commission. Instead, they found their model in the South American countries that emerged from anticommunist military dictatorships in the late 1980s, and where the newly elected leaders lacked either the will or the power to establish their legitimacy on the repudiation of their predecessors' rule. Although they succeeded in instituting truth and reconciliation commissions, and even in enabling the prosecution of former police and military officers, what these incoming governments in South America sought to stigmatize were the abuses committed by representatives of the old regimes rather than the intrinsically criminal nature of these military dictatorships.[81]

In Chile and Argentina, where the military establishments remained largely in place during the respective transitional periods, such a course was clearly dictated by the circumstances. Although the new authorities were intent on strengthening democracy and upholding the rule of law, their first concern was to avoid another coup. They thus settled for the following compromise. On the one hand, Presidents Patricio Aylwin and Raul Alfonsin tried to meet both their moral duty to publicize the plight of individual victims and their legal obligation to investigate individual crimes; on the other hand, they refrained from treating these crimes as the expression of their predecessors' political project. As such, while both granting their citizens' right to the truth and honoring their own commitment to the principle of individual accountability, the Chilean and Argentinean civilian authorities established their reconciliation process on dangerous ground.

In both countries, the new public discourse condemned the crimes of the old regime but called for a reconciliation between friends and foes of the former dictators. The supporters of the former military dictatorships merely had to accept the public exposure of the army's brutal ways. Yet the contention that the threats of chaos and communism justified the suspension of democratic institutions remained a defensible position within the new public discourse. In other words, repudiating such a position was not considered a necessary condition for seeking to reconcile with the people holding the opposite opinion—namely, that a coup against a democratic regime is never justified. Rather than on the repudiation of the previous regime, reconciliation could thus be based on the notion that the end of the cold war had voided the old conflict: in the absence of a communist menace, allies and opponents of the former dictators could now feel equally attached to the sacredness of human rights and merits of democracy.

Although the questionable way in which the Aylwin and Alfonsin governments had reinstated the rule of law accounted for the enduring imperfections of the Chilean and Argentinean democracies, the representatives of the international community had two good reasons for inciting the International War Crimes Tribunals to emulate the South American model of reconciliation. Because it was consistent with the principle of individual accountability, this model enabled Western governments to convey to their public opinion that as the main sponsors of the tribunals, they were living up to their commitments to justice and the worldwide advancement of human rights. At the same time, the South American approach to national reconciliation was consistent with the cultural definition that Western governments sought to project onto post–cold war conflicts, insofar as it required the courts to refrain from incriminating the political regimes that were at the root of these disputes. In spite of the control that the leading members of the international community exercised both on the material means and sensitive information that were put at the disposal of the tribunals, however, the latter, thanks to the courage and persistence of their special prosecutors, succeeded in highlighting exactly what U.S. and European officials wanted them to downplay. Ironically, it is in part the lack of funding and cooperation from Western governments that impelled Louise Arbour and her colleagues to concentrate their work on what they saw as their most important task: tracing the crimes that they were investigating to the political projects from which they stemmed. Consequently, the International War Crimes Tribunals, which were originally meant to serve the doctrine of the international community, turned out to be quite detrimental to its implementation.[82]

Self-Fulfilling Prophecies

One of the most distressing consequences of the policies carried out by the international community was that they managed to produce exactly the kind of situation that they were meant to remedy. In the aftermath of the wars, despite their declared intention to help Bosnians and Rwandans retrieve the truth about their past and take steps toward a democratic future, Western governments were unwilling to assess the impact of their own doctrine both on the course of the conflicts and the prospects faced by the Bosnian and Rwandan societies. In particular, they failed to examine the accuracy of their neocolonial theories about age-old ethnic hatreds and tribal violence, and thus, refused to question the appropriateness of the humanitarian and diplomatic endeavors that were predicated on these premises.

Eager to deny their responsibilities, but also anxious to take full credit for the return of peace, Western governments continued to treat the former protagonists of the Yugoslav and Rwandan conflicts as the representatives of their respective "ethnic" groups, rather than the proponents and opponents of ethnicist regimes. Accordingly, they never honored the Bosnian resistance and liberation of Rwanda by the RPF as the just fights that the international community should have supported but did not. Therefore, it is hardly surprising that instead of vindicating all the Muslims, Croats, Serbs, Tutsis, and Hutus who opposed the murderous racism professed by the supporters of Greater Serbia and Hutu Power, the outcomes of the wars largely heartened the unrepentent advocates of ethnic segregation.

According to the representatives of the international community, the persistent antagonism that continued to suffuse both the former Yugoslav nations and Rwandan communities was not the result of their own policies but the expression of the sectarian agendas pursued by all the local players, including the forces representing the victims of Greater Serbia and Hutu Power. Western officials contended that the foes of Milosevic and Habyarimana were neither motivated by antiracist principles nor championing democracy, but fighting for the interests, and even supremacy, of their own ethnic group. Even as it became increasingly difficult to deny that neither the responsibilities for initiating the violence nor the quantity of atrocities committed during the two wars could be fairly distributed among the various warring factions, the representatives of the international community maintained that the Yugoslav and Rwandan disputes did not deserve a partisan involvement on their part. In their view, neither the ideology nor the human rights record of the Croatian, Bosnian Muslim, and Tutsi leaderships qualified Milosevic and Habyarimana's enemies either as the advocates of a multiethnic citizenry or the protectors of the liberal rule of law.

While it is undeniably true that the democratic credentials of political movements such as Tudjman's Croatian Democratic Community (HDZ), Izetbegovic's Party of Democratic Action (SDA), and Paul Kagame's RPF were—and still are—highly questionable, the real issue is whether an intervention of the international community on their side would have amounted to favoring a sectarian faction over another or whether it would have substantially reduced the level of ethnicist violence, thereby bringing the Balkans and central Africa closer to peace and democracy. In other words, one should wonder whether it was the intrinsic ethnicism of the local players that dictated and justified the alleged impartiality of the international community, or whether it was the unconditional neutrality affected by Western governments and international institutions that enabled the sectarian forces to prevail.

Tudjman, president of Croatia until his death in December 1999, and his party, the HDZ—both the ruling party in Croatia during the Tudjman era and the main political force in Herceg-Bosna—could certainly be described as authoritarian nationalists. In Croatia proper, although the constitution guaranteed political freedom and minority rights, the Tudjman regime was at best a flawed democracy: among other imperfections, the president's party controlled the major media, the government managed to invalidate the results of a municipal election that was unfavorable to the HDZ's candidates, and in 1996, the Parliament passed a law that severely curtailed freedom of the press. As far as the nationalist agenda of the HDZ was concerned, it was deeply disturbing on at least two counts. First, despite the risk of international outrage, the Croatian government took incremental steps toward the rehabilitation of the Ustasha regime of Ante Pavelic.[83] Second, notwithstanding the constitutional provisions protecting minorities, the HDZ rhetoric clearly identified Croatia with its Catholic Croat majority.[84]

In Herceg-Bosna, both the political and human rights records of the Bosnian section of the HDZ and its military branch, the Croatian Defense Council (HVO), are simply appalling: not only did Croatian militias launch a brutal campaign of ethnic cleansing against the Muslim population in the winter of 1993 but even in the aftermath of the peace agreements — that is, the peace treaty of March 1994 between Croats and Muslims, and the Dayton accords of November 1995 — the Bosnian Croat authorities violently resisted the reunification of Mostar — the main city of Herceg-Bosna — and actively opposed the return of Muslim refugees. Judging by their agenda as well as their deeds, it would be difficult to cast Tudjman and his followers as the heroes of an antiethnicist struggle. Still, despite the flaws of the Croatian regime and the crimes of its Hercegovinan protégés, one can argue that if the international community had framed its intervention, in Croatia and Bosnia, as an action against the instigators of the ethnic cleansing campaigns — rather than as a mediation between ethnic factions — such a move would have served the causes of human rights and democracy, in Croatia as well as Bosnia.

Regarding the status and fate of Bosnia-Hercegovina, the Croatian president and his followers oscillated between two strategies. On the one hand, in March 1991, Tudjman and Milosevic held a secret meeting where they planned the ethnic partition of Bosnia. While this first project — which was revived by the two presidents in June 1993 — left some place for a Muslim enclave, it was followed by a second plan — discussed in May 1992 by Karadzic and HVO leader Mate Boban — that envisioned a crude distribution of the spoils of war between Serbia and Croatia. The implementation of this latter project was thus the purpose of the 1993 war launched by the HVO against the Bosnian Muslims. On the other hand, Tudjman presented himself to the international community as the ally, and even the protector, of an independent and multiethnic Bosnia. As such, he successively signed a treaty of political and military cooperation with the Bosnian government in May 1992—two weeks before the meeting between Karadzic and Boban—and more important, the 1994 Washington agreements that established both the Muslim-Croat Federation in Bosnia and the confederation between this entity and the Republic of Croatia.

Although apparently paradoxical, the strategy of the Croatian president is easy to understand: since Western governments were hesitating between making good and reneging on their commitment to the sovereignty of Bosnia, Tudjman wanted to be ready for both options. If the international community was serious about preventing the Serbian troops from realizing their project, his official support for Bosnia's independence would allow him to claim his place among the civilized Western democracies, thereby reaping the political and economic rewards of his righteousness. If the international community decided to let Milosevic get away with Greater Serbia, however, then Tudjman was intent on claiming his right to integrate an ethnically cleansed Herceg-Bosna into a Greater Croatia. In short, in spite of the disturbing similarities between his and Milosevic's ideological agendas, the Croatian president was prepared, albeit for purely opportunistic reasons, to be as respectful of human rights and international law as Western governments would require him to be. He thus ordered his Hercegovinan protégés to fight on the side of the Bosnian army whenever it seemed like the international community was about to oppose the Serbian aggression—specifically, in the first months of the Bosnian War and then in the summer of 1995—and he encouraged them to cleanse Herceg-Bosna of its Muslim population whenever it seemed like Western governments were about to recognize the victory of Milosevic and his followers.

Finally, in Dayton, Tudjman's stance once again mirrored the position of the international community: since the U.S.

arbitrators of the agreements had settled for granting a de jure autonomy to the "Serbian Republic," the Croatian president managed to secure a similar status, albeit de facto, for a Croatian Herceg-Bosna. If Tudjman himself continued to consider Herceg-Bosna a province of Croatia, if the Bosnian Croat authorities still oppose the return of Muslim Hercegovinans to their homes, and if they still flaunt their project to secede from Bosnia and join Croatia, it is fair to say that the conditions of possibility for such unrepentent attitudes were set by the decision of the international community to offer Milosevic both a partial victory in Bosnia and renewed legitimacy as an agent of regional stability. More precisely, it is fair to say that the triumphant ethnicism that still plagues   **97** Herceg-Bosna is not thriving despite the provisions of the Dayton agreements, but largely because of them.

The democratic records of Izetbegovic, the first Bosnian president, and his political party, the SDA, can also be described as wanting. To begin with, in November 1990, after running the first multiparty election in the Yugoslav republic of Bosnia-Herzegovina on a Muslim nationalist platform, the SDA formed a governmental coalition with the two other nationalist parties: the Bosnian Croat HDZ and Karadzic's Serbian Democratic Party (SDS). Together, and despite the growing tensions between their respective militants, the three nationalist parties opposed the so-called citizens' parties—the former Communists, turned social democrats, and the liberal League of Reform Forces—whose mostly urban supporters refused to identify political choice with "ethnic" allegiance.[85]

Furthermore, even though the citizens' parties had called for Bosnia's independence in the referendum of March 1992, in the beginning of the war, the SDA continued to privilege its alliance with the HDZ, despite the need for national unity against the Serbian aggression. In fact, Izetbegovic kept the citizens' parties out of Bosnia's collective presidential body until October 1993, when the Croat-Muslim war and defection of Fikret Abdic in western Bosnia gave him no other choice.[86] In the aftermath of the Dayton Peace Agreement, the president's party has largely confirmed its hegemonic tendencies. Although the SDA has met with strong resistance in the major cities — in Sarajevo and, especially, Tuzla — party officials still occupy powerful positions in the civil administration, media, and army.

Third, in spite of Izetbegovic's repeated commitment to preserve Bosnia's multiethnic society, the actions of his party have sometimes belied his words. In the darkest moments of

the conflict — that is, at the height of the Muslim-Croat War — some prominent members of the SDA inclined toward emulating, or at least surrendering to, the ethnicist visions of their enemies. They embraced the more viable objective of securing the sovereignty of a miniature but purely Muslim state as the dream of a reunited Bosnia seemed to wane. Although Izetbegovic rapidly distanced himself from this project, in the last two years of the struggle, certain segments of the political and military establishment made it clear that their causes were the defense of the Muslim nation and creation of a Muslim state, rather than the survival of a secular and multicultural society. After the war, these SDA hardliners, often with the president's approval, have taken full advantage of the "ethnic" division of the country instituted by the Dayton agreements. They have been able to use the frustration of the refugees — who had good reason to doubt the international community and its professed values — to forward their nationalist and religious agendas. In this way, even though the relatively good results of the citizens' parties in the 1996 and 1998 elections hindered the party's projects, SDA officials have nonetheless succeeded in enforcing a gradual Islamization of the districts under their control.

As both their pre- and postwar records indicate, Izetbegovic and his party were clearly not the perfect champions of
multiculturalism and democracy. Yet, the fact remains that
from 1992 to 1995, the Bosnian authorities were the ones who
organized the resistance and protection of their multiethnic
society against the murderous racism of Milosevic's followers.
Whereas in Banja Luka—the main city of the Serbian Republic—Muslims were forced to wear a white armband, the
Serbian equivalent of the Nazis' yellow star for Jews, before
being either killed or deported, in Sarajevo, Serbs and Croats
fought in the Bosnian army alongside Muslims and held at
least token positions in the Bosnian government. Even if Izetbegovic presented himself to the world as more attached to   **99**
secular democracy than he actually was, even if he overplayed
his commitment to a multiethnic Bosnia in order to enlist the
support of the West, there is still no question that his initial
depiction of the war as a struggle between the proponents and
opponents of ethnic cleansing was largely accurate, especially
compared to the international community's contention that
the conflict pitted ethnic factions acting on their age-old resentments.

As time went by, however, the ethno-cultural definition of
the war that was relentlessly proffered by Western and UN officials slowly became a self-fulfilling prophecy. For more than
three years, the spokespeople for UNPROFOR systematically
blamed "all sides" for the shelling of Bosnian cities by the
Serbian militias: relaying the Serbian propaganda, they went
as far as officially suspecting Bosnian troops of bombing their
own people in order to attract international sympathy. Similarly, for more than three years, Western diplomats referred
to the Bosnians' determination to defend themselves not as
the heroic resistance of a people fighting a genocidal aggression but as the main obstacle to a peace settlement: echoing
Milosevic and Karadzic's frustration, they repeatedly chas-

tised the Bosnian authorities for refusing to capitulate. It is hardly surprising, then, that an increasing number of Bosnian Muslims came to trust those among the SDA officials who not only argued that the values professed by Western democracies needed to be judged by the acts of their representatives but also imputed the chasm between the principles and conduct of the international community to the fact that a majority of Bosnians were Muslims. These contentions were all the more persuasive because SDA hardliners could contrast the betrayals and indifference of the West with the Islamic solidarity demonstrated by Muslim countries, and in particular, by Iran.[87]

In spite of the combined efforts of the international community and the radical wing of the SDA, the portion of Bosnia that remains under the control of Sarajevo's government did not become a Muslim fundamentalist enclave. Still, both the passivity of the West and the obfuscating rhetoric that purported to justify it convinced many Bosnian Muslims that their plight was caricatured precisely because they were Muslims. They came to the conclusion that they could only depend on themselves—on the solidarity of the Muslim community and the strengthening of their Muslim identity—if they were to resist the criminal projects of their former neighbors.

Though certainly understandable, this surge of reactive nationalism could only have dismayed the Bosnians of every descent who fought to preserve a secular and multiethnic society. For the representatives of the international community, however, the postwar evolution of the Bosnian society appeared like a belated vindication of their doctrine. From a practical standpoint, the dominance of nationalist parties in the two Bosnian "entities" was clearly inconvenient for Western governments insofar as it called for the protracted and costly presence of NATO troops on the ground. At the same time, the resolve of the Muslim nationalists, the bitterness of

the secular democrats, and the defiance of the ethnic cleansers—who still control the Serbian Republic and Herceg-
Bosna—all boded quite well for future applications of the
international community's doctrine. Indeed, thanks to the
policies pursued by Western democracies since 1991, there
was a good chance that, next time around, the war in Bosnia
would really look like an ethnic conflict.

As far as Rwanda is concerned, the RPF and its leader, Paul
Kagame, have been the targets of serious accusations regarding their political agenda, Rwanda's carceral and judicial systems, and the record of the Rwandese Patriotic Army (RPA).
First, on the political level, the new rulers were immediately
accused of replacing the old dictatorship of the MRND with
their own brand of authoritarianism.[88] Although the Rwandan government remains nominally pluralist—a number of
posts are still held by Hutus, and most anti–Hutu Power
parties are represented in the cabinet—the critics of the new
regime have relentlessly claimed that the real political power
is exclusively in the hands of the RPF, and that the real power
in the RPF lies with the Tutsi returnees. Moreover, they contend that the RPF leadership's agenda has considerably strayed
from Kagame's original pledge to rebuild Rwanda on the rejection of ethnicist hatred. In its critics' view, the RPF has
become a copy of Burundi's ruling party, the Uprona, which
presents itself as an "ethnic-blind" movement yet uses its
tight control over the army to maintain the supremacy of the
Tutsi minority.

Second, the Rwandan government has been under attack
for its treatment of prisoners. While human rights groups are
the first to emphasize that reconciliation requires justice and
is thus incompatible with impunity, in the case of Rwanda,
they have objected both to the often horrendous conditions
of detention in Rwandan jails—for instance, in 1998, more
than 6,000 people were locked up at Gitarama prison, a place

originally built for 750 prisoners—and to the fact that many arrests were based on scarce evidence. This latter flaw is all the more alarming because of the slowness of the Rwandan justice system. Indeed, in the fall of 1998, only about 1,000 cases had been tried—whereas most of the arrests took place in 1994 and 1995—compared with the 130,000 inmates who were still awaiting trial.[89]

In addition, since the RPF conquered Kigali, the Rwandese Patriotic Army has been accused of committing massive human rights violations. Wartime atrocities notwithstanding, the first major massacre took place in 1995, when Rwandan troops disbanded the UN-run refugee camp of Kibeho, in the southwestern part of the country: although UN workers who witnessed the event reported that many of the victims were either stampeded by their panicking peers or killed by the Interahamwe militia in the camp that wanted to keep the civilians as shields, they also accused the RPA of shooting indiscriminately at the fleeing refugees.[90] The second, and most horrendous, massacre attributed to the Rwandan army took place during the campaign that brought Laurent Kabila to power in the ex-Zaire. In the winter of 1996–1997, along with Kabila's forces, Rwandan troops destroyed all remaining UN refugee camps in the Kivu region. While more than half a million Hutus—those who were still in the camps when the RPA overtook them—were allowed to return peacefully to Rwanda, the June 1998 report of the UN's SGIT states that the refugees who had fled the camps before the RPA's offensive were chased by the Rwandan troops, and that as many as 100,000 of them might have been slaughtered.

Fourth, since 1997, the Rwandan armed forces have been decried for conducting brutal reprisals in northwestern Rwanda—in the region of Ruhengeri and Gisenyi, which is both Habyarimana's birthplace and a Hutu Power stronghold—against the Hutu villagers whom they accuse of protecting remnants of the Interahamwe militias and ex-FAR. Too weakened to wage a full-scale war, the surviving perpetrators of the genocide have nonetheless remained powerful enough to raid the communities of Tutsi returnees and Congolese Tutsi refugees who settled near the Congolese border.[91] True to their old methods, they not only seek to exterminate Tutsis but also to implicate the local Hutu population in their activities. The villagers have once again been coerced, or at least coaxed, into taking part in the massacres. Faced with this resurgence of Hutu Power strategy, the Rwandan army has gone back and forth between viewing the local Hutu communities as the militias' hostages and treating them as their accomplices. While the former position has impelled the RPA to involve Hutu villagers in mandatory campaigns of moral and political reeducation, the latter has translated into the systematic destruction of Hutu villages.[92]

Finally, the occupation of a large portion of the Congo by the RPA, since November 1996, has deeply damaged the army's reputation. In response to those who accuse Kigali of nurturing imperialistic ambitions, Kagame keeps insisting that Rwandan troops never had any other motives for staying in the Democratic Republic of the Congo than the security of their own country and safety of the Congolese Tutsis—since Interahamwe militias have never ceased to operate from the Congolese territory. From the standpoint of the local population, however, Rwandan forces are merely perceived as brutal and predatory colonizers whose main objective is to occupy at least the eastern half of the Congo and claim a lion's share of the country's natural resources.

The record of the Rwandan government may well be as bad as its detractors say it is. In other words, it may be true that the Rwandan regime has progressively become a military dictatorship whose main preoccupations are the protection of a dominant Tutsi minority and de facto annexation of the Kivu province. Yet, in Rwanda as in Bosnia, the international community and its doctrine must be held at least partly responsible for this unfortunate evolution. In the immediate aftermath of the genocide, Western governments and UN agencies were certainly eager to display their compassion for the victims of yet another African tragedy. Nevertheless, their main concern was to minimize the exposure of their own negligence, both before and during the spring of 1994. They thus had little interest in helping the Rwandan government perform its most urgent task: investigating and establishing the course of events that led to the systematic genocidal slaughter of almost one million people in a little more than three months.

Under the rule of Habyarimana's immediate successors, Hutus who refused to participate in the annihilation of their Tutsi friends and neighbors were perceived as RPF collaborators who needed to be executed. Consequently, when Kagame and his troops entered Kigali, almost every surviving Rwandan who was neither a Tutsi nor a so-called moderate Hutu—a traitor to the Hutu Power cause—was likely to have been an executioner of the genocide. To complicate matters even more, within less than a year after the former rebels took office, about three-quarters of a million Tutsis from the diaspora settled in Rwanda. Like the cadres of the RPF, most of them were the children of exiles and had never lived in their own country. The job of the new government was thus to organize the peaceful coexistence, in a completely devastated land, of three vastly heterogeneous groups of people: defeated but not necessarily remorseful murderers, surviving but not necessarily forgiving victims, and eager but necessarily dislocated newcomers.

To succeed in this momentous endeavor, the Rwandan authorities certainly needed all the help they could get, and not only in the form of humanitarian aid and economic assistance.

For if the people who had killed and the people whose families and friends had been killed were to live side by side—and if the victorious Tutsi returnees were to seek reconciliation with, rather than domination over, the Hutu majority—the first priority of the Rwandan government had to be the stigmatization of the monstrous ideology and implacable political organization that had been the causes of the killing. In other words, if collective vengeance against the Hutus was to be avoided, nothing could be more urgent than to expose the crimes of Hutu Power: for only an officially proclaimed distinction between the Hutu community and the regime that had committed a genocide in its name would at once allow the former to disassociate itself from the latter—albeit in hindsight—and dissuade the Tutsi survivors from confusing revenge with retribution. Therefore, what the RPF and its allies most needed from the international community was twofold: they wanted its representatives to acknowledge the nature of Rwanda's plight—that the genocide committed by the proponents of Hutu Power was precisely what the victors of Nazism had pledged to ban forever; and they wanted to be provided with the means of establishing national reconstruction in the quest for justice. But the international community offered neither the symbolic nor material support that the Rwandan government so crucially needed.

As soon as the RPF single-handedly put an end to the genocide, the world's compassion focused on the two million Hutus that the Interahamwe militias and routed FAR had forced to flee, first to the Turquoise security zone in southern Rwanda and then to the refugee camps in eastern Zaire. Of course, the representatives of the international community knew full well that a sizable proportion of these people were either the organizers or more or less willing executioners of the genocide. Yet, for about two years, both the media attention and humanitarian activity provoked by the Rwandan tragedy were purposefully centered on the refugees rather than the devastation that they had left behind.

French peacekeepers and UN officials, as the successive managers of the camps, did not have exactly the same motives for directing the world's compassion toward the Hutu refugees. The officers in charge of operation Turquoise had a clear political stake in presenting their Hutu Power protégés as the victims of the conflict. Although they did not dare claim that the refugees were innocent victims, French authorities nonetheless suggested that two million people would not have fled their homes in such haste unless they had good reason to fear for their lives.[93] As for the UN officials who took over the camps

after operation Turquoise ended, their main preoccupation was with restoring their institution's image: eager to replace the memory of UNAMIR's shameful exit during the genocide with a fresh display of humanitarian solicitude, they knew that the latter not only required devoted aid workers but also grateful recipients. They thus decided to concentrate their efforts on the camps, thinking that frustrated criminals and their hapless pawns would make the UN High Committee for Refugees look better than would reproachful survivors.

Whether motivated by the political interests of the French government or the UN's desire to save face, the official representation of the Rwandan tragedy as a refugee crisis plainly amounted to a denial of the genocide. Yet the irresponsibility of the international community did not stop there: the actual management of the camps, even after Turquoise ended, seemed to aim at nothing less than giving the proponents of Hutu Power a second chance to accomplish their goal. Indeed, between the summer of 1994 and fall of 1996, the organizers of the genocide who had settled in the camps were not only free, protected, and fed by the international community; they were also allowed to keep their weapons—as well as buy new ones—train, and run the camps in exactly the same fashion as they had run Rwanda. In short, they were given free license to kill, both within and outside UN facilities.

Inside the camps, the Hutu Power leadership was allowed to intimidate and even execute anyone who expressed the desire to go back to Rwanda. Although the Rwandan government insisted that the Hutu refugees could safely come home—and even though the UN office in Kigali confirmed that the Hutus who had returned were safe—the UN workers managing the camps not only failed to denounce the terror imposed by the Hutu Power militias but also largely echoed the contention that Hutus would not voluntarily go back to Rwanda as long as the RPF was in power. More important, UN officials did nothing to stop the revamped militias from launching murderous raids from the camps. These attacks first targeted Tutsis in Rwanda, since the Zairean camps were only a few miles from the border, but soon involved the 400,000 Zairean Tutsis—for the most part, longtime immigrants of Rwandan origin—who lived in the Kivu province. In addition, once the Hutu militias started mounting operations in southern Kivu—where a latent tension already existed between the relatively affluent Tutsis known as Banyamulenge and the rest of the population—the Zairean troops, encouraged by the impunity granted to the "refugees," increasingly joined forces with them. Thus, by 1996, the massacres perpetrated by the proponents of Hutu Power were once again reaching horrendous proportions.

Faced with an impending full-scale war of even wider dimensions than the genocidal conflict of 1994—since Zairean Tutsis and Zairean troops were now involved—the Rwandan government repeatedly asked the international community representatives to disarm the Hutu militias, arrest their leaders, and let the rest of the refugees go home. But Western governments and UN officials refused to either police the camps or even attempt to separate the civilians from the militias.

Their excuse, once again, was that a forceful intervention in the camps would put the lives of the humanitarian workers at risk. Determined to deny that their management of the refugee camps was paving the way for a second genocide, the representatives of the international community countered the indignant protests of the Rwandan authorities by both congratulating themselves for the humanitarian accomplishments of the UN High Committee for Refugees and emphasizing the human rights violations committed by the RPF-led government.

The mix of passivity, hypocrisy, and self-righteousness displayed by the representatives of the international community produced its usual effects. On the one hand, the fact that the proponents of Hutu Power were allowed to prepare for their big counteroffensive in the camps of Zaire could not be ignored by the four million Hutus who had stayed in Rwanda. Because so many of them had been implicated in the genocide, either as killers or at least witnesses, the prospect of Hutu Power's imminent return made them equally apprehensive of RPF's justice and being reported as RPF collaborators once their old rulers were back. Therefore, a majority of Hutus were understandably inclined to await the restoration of the old regime rather than cooperate with the new authorities. On the other hand, the fact that the international community was at once reducing the genocide of the Tutsis to a humanitarian crisis—that is, a situation where victims abound but victimizers are conspicuously absent—and enabling its organizers to regroup was bound to affect both the agenda and methods of the RPF. Although Kagame and his associates continued to claim that their ultimate goal was to free Rwanda from a century of ethnicist policies, what they saw as their most urgent mission was to secure the survival of the Zairean as well as Rwandan Tutsis by all means necessary. And indeed, such means turned out to include the invasion of a foreign country, summary executions of thousands of Hutu refugees, and increasingly authoritarian control over the Hutu majority in Rwanda.

Convinced that neither the UN nor Western governments would prevent its enemies from exterminating its people, the RPF leadership took it on itself to disband the camps and eradicate Hutu Power. To the amazement of the international community, the Rwandan forces, along with their Ugandan allies, succeeded: not only did they both ward off the threat of a second genocide and repatriate the vast majority of Hutu refugees but they also managed to topple Mobutu, replacing him with a man, Kabila, who owed them his ascent to power. Yet, spectacular as it was, the success of the Rwandan government could only be interpreted as a victory for the Tutsis. Indeed, regardless of the antiracist rhetoric of the RPF, there was no denying that both Rwanda and its giant neighbor, the freshly renamed Democratic Republic of the Congo, were now ruled by an almost exclusively Tutsi army. While the sudden surge of the RPA to regional dominance earned the Rwandan government considerably more Western support than its legitimate claims of the previous years, it also contributed to the polarization of central Africa along "ethnic" lines. The imperial position of the Tutsi-led RPA could not help but fuel fresh anti-Tutsi sentiments throughout the region, and in turn, this renewed hostility reinforced the conviction of the RPF leadership that Tutsis needed to be in a position of political power and military superiority in order to guarantee their own safety.[94] In short, true to its self-fulfilling capacities, the doctrine of the international community had been instrumental yet again not in remedying an ethnic conflict but in creating one.

Though it proved disastrous from the perspective of the societies to which it was applied, for several years, the international community's doctrine acted as a virtuous circle for those who had devised it. Initially, Western powers defined post–cold war disputes as ethnic wars because such a view enabled them to justify the limitation of their own intervention to humanitarian missions and neutral mediations. Yet, in time, they were able to use the results of their persistent "impartiality" to rationalize their initial position. In other words, the misleading diagnoses of the conflicts that Western governments originally put forward to lower their costs ended up being partially vindicated by the continued administration of their low-cost policies. Despite ample evidence that they not only mismanaged the Yugoslav and Rwandan crises but also purposefully misrepresented them, the leading members of the international community were not particularly inclined to mend a doctrine that had proved so cost effective.

An Ambiguous Evolution

A slow but important evolution took place during the second half of the 1990s. While the discourse proffered in the name of the international community remained largely the same, the practices that went along with these familiar words gradually strayed from the supposedly impartial humanitarianism and evenhanded diplomacy characteristic of the years 1991 to 1995. In Bosnia, even though Western and UN officials continued to both complain about the sectarian nationalism of all the formerly warring parties and call for a process of reconciliation based on mutual forgiveness, they nonetheless applied an increasingly contrasted treatment—in terms of political pressure as well as economic assistance—to the Muslim-Croat Federation and the Serbian entity known as Republika Srpska.[95] Similarly, in central Africa, while the representatives of the international community continued to obfuscate the truth about the Rwandan genocide in order to minimize their own responsibilities, some of them—particularly the United States—compensated for their persistent denial by providing crucial diplomatic and military assistance to the Rwandan government. In 1996–1997, U.S. officials not only supported Kagame's—and Museveni's—plan to topple Mobutu and replace the old Zairean dictator with Kabila; they also helped Kigali cover up the atrocities perpetrated by the Rwandan army during its first campaign in the former Zaire. Then, in the summer of 1998, the Clinton administration condoned, albeit covertly, the second Congolese war launched by the Rwandan and Ugandan leaders, this time against the Kabila regime.[96] Finally, in July 1999, U.S. diplomats saw to it that Rwandan interests were met by the peace plan signed in Lusaka, which involved the various countries implicated in the Congolese conflict.[97]

What these discreetly yet decidedly "partial" practices mainly reflected was a change of leadership among the authorized voices of the international community. First, as already mentioned, in the aftermath of the Dayton accord and the victory of the RPF in Rwanda, the United States emerged as the only influential Western power in the Balkans as well as central Africa. Second, the politicians and diplomat who had shaped the doctrine of the international community and advocated for its rigorous application—namely, Mitterrand, Major, and Boutros-Ghali—all left the scene between 1995 and 1997. Their three successors, furthermore, each had a motive for modifying the policies of the international community: Chirac, who did not share Mitterrand's conviction that France should support Serbia in order to balance the German-Croat alliance, developed a strong animosity toward Milosevic's regime;[98] Annan, whose record as the head of the UN peacekeeping agency had been tainted by the failure of UNAMIR, needed to gain some credibility with African leaders; and as for Blair, he gradually positioned himself as the main proponent of a Western alliance that would act, if necessary on its own, in the name of human rights and the rule of law, and for the sake of a democratic international community in the making.

Third, within the Clinton administration, both the tone and substance of U.S. foreign policy were inflected—at least

vis-à-vis the former Yugoslavia and central Africa—by the appointment of Albright as secretary of state. In her former capacity as U.S. ambassador to the UN during Clinton's first term, Albright had vainly raised the specter of the Munich debacle of 1938 in order to toughen the stance of the international community regarding the ethnic cleansing campaigns launched by Milosevic and his followers. Yet, at the same time, the future secretary of state also played a major role in Washington's deliberate attempts to deny the existence of the Rwandan genocide. Therefore, once at the State Department, the combination of frustration and guilt that she derived from her UN experience impelled Albright to take some distance from the policies of appeasement and obfuscation character-   **113**
istic of the previous years. To convince her colleagues and allies to change course, the secretary of state could argue that in the long run, the self-fulfilling properties of the doctrine associated with the international community would turn out to be less felicitous than anticipated. On the one hand, there was admittedly a good chance that the vengeful bitterness often demonstrated by the victims of ethnic cleansing and genocide would act as a retroactive justification of the "impartial," and thus limited, involvement of the West in post–cold war conflicts. On the other hand, the growing weariness of the Western public with the alleged powerlessness of the international community might eventually pressure the latter's leading members into costlier and lengthier interventions—such as NATO's in Bosnia–than if its representatives had given early support to the local foes of racist political forces. Hence the belated turn of U.S. foreign policy toward strengthening Washington's ties with the Bosnian authorities in Sarajevo and the RPF-led government in Kigali.

While Albright and Blair's efforts succeeded in partially altering the ways of the international community, the discourse used by Western and UN officials remained remarkably unchanged until the spring of 1999. What dissuaded the representatives of the international community from reassessing their early depictions of post–cold war disputes was first and foremost their determination to protect their past record. Having based their entire strategy on the premise that post–cold war conflicts stemmed from the cultural backwardness of the communities involved, they could not suddenly recognize the political character of the Yugoslav and Rwandan wars without exposing their own responsibilities in the ethnic cleansing campaigns launched by Milosevic and the genocide planned by the Hutu Power regime. Thus, since the persistent application of their doctrine had arguably vindicated their early claims about the intractability of old ethnic hatreds, Western leaders — especially those who were already in power during the Bosnian and Rwandan wars — were understandably even less inclined to revise their discourse than their practices.

The leading members of the international community had yet another reason for keeping the same rhetoric. In this case, what was at stake did not involve concealing a deplorable record but averting a momentous precedent. Though their motives were different, European authorities — with the exception of Blair's government — and the U.S. military were both particularly wary of an international discourse that would be explicitly informed by the memory of Munich and critique of appeasement policies. For the members of the European Union, the trouble with an international community officially intent on substituting partisan interventionism for impartial diplomacy was that it would immediately underscore the absence of a credible European defense and consequently deepen Europe's dependency on the United States. For the Pentagon, but also for the isolationist wings of both the Republican and Democratic Parties, a doctrine implying that the lives of U.S. soldiers might be risked whenever massive human rights violations were committed in some foreign land against a foreign population obviously stood in stark contradiction with the army's conception of national security. The State Department found it more expedient to convince the Pentagon to provide training and assistance to the RPA and Bosnian army than to insist that the United States and its allies publicly declare that preventing ethnicist regimes from implementing their criminal program was among the most pressing political priorities of the international community.

For the U.S. government and its partners—primarily South Africa in central Africa and the British in the Balkans—this combination of more partisan practices with an unmodified discourse purported to widen the scope of tactical moves at their disposal. According to the circumstances, they could either revert back to a strict application of their doctrine, affect to do so while secretly assisting one of the parties, or even openly support one side but for the ostensible purpose of leveling the field.[99] Yet, the discrepancy between the original discursive strategy of the international community and the new policies that were applied under its guise also produced serious perverse effects.

What the political forces that were now the recipients of the State Department's solicitude felt they had to provide in exchange for U.S. diplomatic and military support was less a credible commitment to democracy and human rights for the future than a pledge to remain silent about the past record of their new protectors. In the case of Rwanda especially, the Clinton administration compensated for sparing itself the pain of reassessing its role during the genocide by endowing the RPF-led government with the means of satisfying its political and economic ambitions in the Democratic Republic of the Congo. Indeed, Kigali's official motives for backing the rebellion against Kabila—namely, protecting Rwanda's borders against Interahamwe raids and preventing pogroms of

Congolese Tutsis—were not merely pretexts.[100] Yet the Rwandan government also saw its second campaign in the Congo as a way of establishing a de facto protectorate in the eastern provinces of that country.[101] By supporting the RPF too late and in exchange for its silence, rather than as the antiracist force that the United States failed to help during the genocide, U.S. officials enabled the Rwandan authorities to invoke the danger of a second genocide in order to forward their predatory interests.

As well, the former beneficiaries of the "impartial" approach prescribed by the doctrine of the international community failed to appreciate the evolution of the Western leaders' policies. This was particularly the case with Milosevic, who, understandably misled by the familiar rhetoric of his Western interlocutors—as well as by the leeway that their ostensible evenhandedness continued to give him—could not foresee that his days as a tough-yet-indispensable agent of regional stability were numbered.[102] In other words, the Serbian leader fell prey to the growing gap between what the representatives of the international community still needed to say in order to ward off embarrassing questions and exaggerated expectations, and what they could no longer afford to do without alienating their public opinion. While it prolonged the crisis and proved extremely costly for the Kosovars, Milosevic's misconception about the predicament of his future enemies was hardly imputable to him. Rather, it showed the limitations and dangers of what could be called the amended doctrine of the international community. At the same time, however, Milosevic's confusion produced its own set of "perverse" effects since it eventually compelled Western officials to modify their discourse.

An Unsettling Message

nsofar as its persistent application created the conditions on which it was predicated, the doctrine of the international community acted as a virtuous circle. Judging by its effects on the peoples of the Balkans and central Africa, however, one should add that the doctrine's virtuosity merely concerned the relationship between Western governments and their constituents. In this respect, it is indeed noteworthy that the perspective developed by the international community in the post–cold war era raised much less opposition than the ideologies of the preceding period. This absence of outrage could be explained, to a certain extent, by the relative indifference that the Western public traditionally manifests for foreign conflicts that do not reflect domestic issues. Yet even the European and U.S. citizens who were critical of their leaders' inability to stave off the brutal struggles of the post–cold war era seemed to lack a clear political perspective from which to question the doctrine of the international community.

During the cold war, the abuses committed in the name of the Free World had two kinds of critics within the Western public: liberals who reproached their governments for not living up to their values, and leftist radicals who condemned

Western powers for enacting their imperialist agenda. Certainly, the two types of critics entertained vastly different hopes. Western liberals, convinced of the intrinsic worth of their system of governance, merely wished that their leaders would reform, while radicals saw Western capitalism as the main cause of oppression in the world and, thus, longed for revolutionary change. Yet, despite their diverging aspirations, both groups shared the same indignation regarding their governments' support for anticommunist dictators, especially when this support amounted to fomenting coups against democratically elected leaders such as Mohammed Mossadegh in Iran, Patrice Lumumba in the Congo, and Salvador Allende in Chile, to name only a few. Whether motivated by faith in Western liberalism or aversion to Western imperialism, the reformist and revolutionary Left could thus agree on a common demand: that Western powers let the peoples of the developing world choose their own political representatives.

With the end of the cold war, the association of the Western Left with a "dovish" stance, while still the expected norm, gradually lost some of its clarity. Already during the Gulf War, a certain malaise was perceptible in both the liberal and radical camps. Liberals were torn between their sense that operation Desert Storm was nothing more than a traditional imperialist campaign aimed at maintaining Western control over the price of oil and their inability to deny that the official motivations of the nascent international community were in conformity with a liberal agenda. Indeed, as already mentioned, the ostensible purpose of the Gulf War was to repel the aggression of a sovereign nation by one of its neighbors, and the general framework in which Desert Storm was supposed to take place was a new world order based on respect for international law and devoted to promoting the rule of law. The radical Left, for its part, did not have any qualms about denouncing the U.S.-led operation. Yet its members could neither build up Hussein as a hero of the anti-imperialist struggle nor articulate what they saw as the proper response to the expansionist plans of regional dictators who were no longer useful to their cold war patrons but still possessed the arsenal once bestowed on them either by the United States and its European allies or the Soviet Union. Even if the radical critics of the Gulf War had no problem exposing the cynicism and hypocrisy of Western leaders, they were nonetheless reduced to framing their outrage in a weak pacifist discourse—that peace is always better than war—rather than from an emancipatory perspective. They thus failed to offer a credible political challenge to the new world order rhetoric developed by Western governments.

Although unsettling for both wings of the Western Left, the Gulf War still presented its opponents with a familiar picture: a Western alliance imposing its will on a Third World country and sacrificing the lives of innocent civilians to the economic interests of multinational oil companies. Far more disturbing for the ideological comfort of the Western Left were the objections raised about the way in which Western powers handled the Yugoslav and Rwandan crises. Certainly, the fact that the international community, despite the end of the cold war, was unable—or worse, unwilling—to avert two genocidal wars could only call for outrage. But neither radicals nor liberals could fully endorse the critique offered by the detractors of the post–cold war doctrine tested in the Balkans and central Africa.

For the radical wing of the Western Left, this critique presented a problem because it was not primarily motivated by an ideological opposition to Western hegemony. Contrary to the "anti-imperialist" militants who mobilized against the Gulf War, the mix of scholars, journalists, humanitarian organizations, and human rights groups that took the interna-

tional community to task for its policies in the former Yugoslavia and Rwanda did not fault Western governments for
imposing some new world order onto non-Western populations. Indeed, far from accusing the international community
of meddling abusively in the affairs of sovereign countries,
they blamed its leading members for not intervening enough,
or at least not appropriately, in the conflicts generated by the
end of the cold war.

Yet, these activists, scholars, and journalists posed no less
of a problem for the liberal wing of the Western Left—even
though they themselves were, for the most part, traditional
Western liberals [103]—insofar as they did not merely complain
about the lack of cohesiveness and resolve demonstrated by
Western powers and international institutions. In fact, far
from simply asking that Western governments do more for the
victims of "ethnic violence"—more humanitarian aid, more
diplomatic efforts, more money for reconstruction, and so
forth—they exposed the impeccably liberal doctrine proudly
proffered by the international community as a neocolonial
perspective aimed at justifying Western inaction in the face
of genocide and ethnic cleansing.

Eager to adapt their hostility to Western foreign policy
to the conditions of the post–cold war era, the heirs of the
old anti-imperialist Left might have been persuaded to rally
against a doctrine predicated on the "tribalization" of non-
Western societies. They could hardly be expected, however, to
endorse a critique of this doctrine that stigmatized a Western-
led international community for failing to mount forceful and
politically driven interventions in post–cold war conflicts. For
regardless of who they actually held responsible for the Rwandan genocide or Bosnian War, militants whose political lives
had been largely defined by their antipathy for Western hegemony were not likely to put themselves in the position of wel-
coming a military action sponsored by the U.S. government

and its Western European allies. From a strictly logical stand-point, there was certainly no reason to assume that having op-posed the Gulf War should have prevented anyone from advo-cating a confrontational stance vis-à-vis Milosevic's followers or Hutu Power militias. Yet most Western radicals nonethe-less thought it wise to remain discreet, if not totally silent, about Bosnia and Rwanda in order to preserve the purity of their anti-imperialist agenda.

While the end of the cold war put Western radicals on the defensive, it initially gave liberals the hope that the demise of Communism would entice their governments to adopt a principled foreign policy. Eager to see Western democracies deploy more efforts, and even take more risks, to foster de-mocratization and protect human rights worldwide, most Western liberals were understandably dismayed by the record of the international community in the former Yugoslavia and Rwanda. Still, despite their frustration, they could not have been expected to trace their leaders' failings to a doctrine purported to curb ethnic violence by facilitating a society's transition from the tribal rule of blood to the liberal rule of law. Insofar as they had already been torn between support-ing the Gulf War on the basis of its legal justification and op-posing a new world order that would require such a carnage, liberals were tempted to welcome the prospect of an inter-national community acting less as world police, and more as an agent of humanitarian relief, patient diplomacy, and con-ciliatory solutions. Of course, there is once again no reason to assume that having winced at the portrayal of the Gulf War as a liberal crusade against a new Hitler should have pre-vented anyone from comparing the political agendas devel-oped by the proponents of Greater Serbia and Hutu Power to the program of the Nazis. But most Western liberals thought it wise to merely deplore the "powerlessness" of the interna-tional community in the face of "ethnic violence," rather than question their governments' motives for "depoliticizing" the crimes committed by racist regimes.

At odds with both wings of the Western Left — and needless to say, no more in harmony with the preoccupations of the Right[104] — the scholars, journalists, and activists who denounced the post–cold war doctrine found themselves in a paradoxical position. Certainly, they managed to make themselves visible and even relatively popular. Some of the writers — reporters as well as academics — whose accounts of the Bosnian and Rwandan crises portrayed the action of the international community in the most scathing terms were widely acclaimed — critically at least — for their courage and lucidity. As for humanitarian organizations such as Doctors without Borders and human rights groups such as Human Rights Watch, they are probably among the most celebrated — at least by the Western media and public opinion — heroes of the post–cold war era.

At the same time, these writers and activists were largely unable to advance their cause. Although their accounts of the Yugoslav and Rwandan wars effectively contributed to discrediting the action of the international community, they nonetheless failed to undermine the doctrine on which this action was based. The main reason was not that their arguments were inconclusive or unclear, but, as we have seen, that they disrupted familiar ideological frameworks, especially within the Western Left. Confronted with the alleged powerlessness of the international community with regard to ethnic cleansing and genocide, liberals could hardly envision that a doctrine that was music to their ears was in fact part of the problem, while radicals could not accept that pressuring Western governments into intervening militarily might be part of the solution.

In other words, the unsettling effects of their critique prevented the detractors of the international community from creating the political conditions under which they could persuasively convey the following claims. First, that the cause of post–cold war conflicts was not the return of ancient ethnic hatreds but the ethnicist turn taken by political regimes whose survival was threatened by the fall of the Berlin Wall. Given this, by tribalizing these conflicts, the leading members of the international community sought to minimize the cost of their involvement while still pretending to honor their commitment to human rights and the rule of law. Third, the humanitarian and supposedly impartial stance of the international community, which was predicated on the tribalization of post–cold war conflicts, not only enabled the instigators of these wars to implement their ethnicist agenda but also enticed the representatives of their victims to defend themselves with similar means. And thus, while ethnic hatred was not the cause of post–cold war conflicts, it ended up being the main consequence of the policies applied by the international community.

An Emerging Polarization

For most of the 1990s, both the liberal and radical wings of the Western Left were unwilling to either condone the doctrine of the international community or fully endorse the charges of its critics. But while they were equally incapable of taking a firm position on how to address post–cold war conflicts, liberals were undeniably more unsettled than radicals by the persistent inaction of Western governments in the face of ethnic cleansing and genocide. From the perspective of a convalescent anti-imperialist Left, the failures of the West in Bosnia and Rwanda were nothing less than a blessing in disguise, strategically at least, insofar as they exposed the blatant fallacy of the liberal expectations raised by the end of the cold war. Indeed, the pusillanimity of the international community exemplified by the Bosnian and Rwandan crises demonstrated that the world of the 1990s, though governed by the triumphant West, was hardly a place where the globalization of the market economy was fostering democracy or encouraging the entire planet to uphold human and civil rights. What the doctrine of the international community underscored instead was the stark contrast between the flawless resolve demonstrated by Western powers in submitting what used to be the Second and Third Worlds to the iron rules of good governance—that is, an economic policy based on free trade, untaxed movements of capital, and budgetary restraint—and their alleged powerlessness when confronted with genocide and ethnic cleansing. Although anti-imperialist intellectuals and activists had little to say about the type of international action that post–cold war disputes would require, they could at least rely on the mismanagement of these situations by the representatives of the international community in order to discredit the moral and political justification advanced by the proponents of unhinged capitalism—namely, that there was a necessary link between economic laissez-faire and the progress of human rights and democracy.

In contrast, Western liberals gradually came to perceive the alleged powerlessness of the international community as a curse that threatened to destroy the hopes raised by the end of the cold war. In the first years following the fall of the Berlin Wall, principled liberals had already seen their expectations shaken by the way in which Western governments were handling their victory. Irked by the moral pretenses that had surrounded the Gulf War, they were also deeply troubled by the social toll that capitalist globalization was taking on the developing world and, to a lesser extent, developed countries. Therefore, if they were to retain anything of their enthusiasm of the late 1980s, Western liberals could not let their governments get away with merely expressing helpless indignation in the face of genocide and crimes against humanity.

For the representatives of the anti-imperialist Left, the human rights record of the international community was a secondary concern. Their main purpose in underscoring its flaws was to show that the social and economic domination of the West had no redeeming features. Conversely, Western liberals, who were inclined to repress their anxieties about the devastating effects of economic globalization, considered the regional and local conflicts that their governments imputed to ancient ethnic hatreds as the ultimate challenge to their liberal faith. Consequently, even though the radical and liberal Lefts pursued two potentially conflicting agendas, on the whole, they managed to largely ignore each other throughout the 1990s—at least until the spring of 1999.

Anti-imperialist militants spent most of the decade waiting for a big financial crash. In the meantime, they devoted their energy to denouncing what they saw as the "other side" of the international community, namely, a global strategy that was masterminded by the U.S. administration and its closest allies, and whose aims included opening markets for Western goods, services, and capital, supplying Western societies with cheap natural resources, and lowering the cost of labor worldwide. The primary means through which this strategy was implemented consisted of pressuring the governments of poorer countries into submitting to the dictates of the International Monetary Fund (IMF), World Bank, and World Trade Organization (WTO)—the much more directive and comprehensive successor to the General Agreement on Tariffs and Trade—and demonizing the regimes intent on challenging the rules of good governance.

During the early 1990s, radical activists suffered both from the ideological hegemony of their opponents and the political persuasion of some of their objective allies. In the West, while unemployment in Europe and the increasing "flexibility" of the conditions of labor, especially in the United States, kept workers weak and disorganized, the populist and neofascist Rights further deepened the morass of the Left by joining their voices to the anti-imperialist critique of globalization. Similarly, in developing countries, the strongest charges against Western neocolonialism came from nationalist despots and faltering exponents of crony capitalism. As the specter of financial crises began to haunt the markets formerly known as emerging, however, the social ills engendered by the process of economic globalization increased skepticism about the virtues of unregulated capitalism—including in the West—and thus gave renewed buoyancy and credibility to anti-imperialist stances. Still too shaken by the outcome of the cold war to review, let alone revive, their revolutionary hopes, Western radicals settled for what could be described as a Keynesian critique of globalization. Their main charge against the financial and economic pressure jointly exercised by the IMF and WTO was that it deprived the people, or at least its legitimate representatives, of the fundamental attributes of its sovereignty. In other words, allowing the IMF and WTO to enforce their respective criteria of economic soundness and commercial fairness amounted to putting unelected bodies in control of the budgetary and fiscal tools that should have enabled national governments to shape the social policies of their countries. According to the anti-imperialist Left, then, the actual dictatorship exercised by these international institutions simply made a mockery of the democratic values allegedly promoted by the leading members of the international community.

In spite of the growing resentment encountered by the model of good governance defined by the IMF, Western liberals continued to claim that the market economy was necessary for economic growth and political freedom. Though they were quick to add that capitalism was hardly a sufficient condition for prosperity and democracy, the liberal contribution to the critique of globalization rarely went further than wishing that the flows of international commerce and circulation of capital would eventually be balanced by a parallel globalization of social justice. Nevertheless, what drew increasingly bitter complaints from committed liberals was the discrepancy that they perceived between their governments' unwavering determination on the issue of economic freedom and the affected powerlessness of the international community with respect to the protection of human rights and advancement of democracy. While they could not quite decide between the arguments that Western political leaders advanced to justify their policies—since these contentions seemed impeccably liberal—and the charges made by the critics of the international community—who for the most part, were themselves liberals—the liberal wing of the Western Left still spent most of the 1990s asking that their governments do for their professed values what they did for their material interests.

Until March 1999, in short, liberals focused on post–cold war conflicts and kept a low profile on globalization, while radicals railed against the unprecedented economic imperialism of the West and evoked the flaws of the international community for the sole purpose of exposing the hypocrisy of its leading members. But with NATO's intervention in Kosovo, the "peaceful coexistence"—in the cold war sense of the phrase—between liberals and anti-imperialists came to an abrupt end. Whereas the doctrine of the international community had kept the two wings of the Western Left out of each other's way, the discourse used by NATO powers to justify operation Allied Force had the immediate effect of pitting liberals and radicals against one another.

On the liberal side, the war against Serbia succeeded in dissipating a ten-year-old malaise. Indeed, thanks to the new-found determination demonstrated by their governments, all liberals could now wholeheartedly agree, albeit in hindsight, with the small group of intellectuals and activists who had denounced the doctrine of the international community in Bosnia and Rwanda. In other words, once their leaders declared that democracies had a duty to oppose genocidal regimes, Western liberals stopped denying that the leading members of the international community had previously engaged in a deliberate strategy of appeasement. What this be-lated acknowledgment purported to convey was that NATO's air campaign against Serbia constituted a momentous prece-dent, especially since it had happened practically at the same time as Pinochet's arrest in London. Henceforth, liberals thus asserted, the representatives of the international community would no longer feel entitled to invoke exaggerated notions of national sovereignty and fallacious conceptions of regional stability in order to escape their own obligation to prevent massive human rights violations. In some liberal circles, the optimism generated by NATO's resolve and Milosevic's capitu-lation even produced a renewed faith in the virtuous circle, promised by the victors of the cold war, between the globaliza-tion of the market economy and the advancement of human rights and democracy.

No less a turning point on the anti-imperialist side, NATO's intervention in Kosovo impelled most Western radicals to make the purity of their cause an absolute priority, thereby giving it precedence over the moral revulsion that Milosevic's policies inspired in them. As already mentioned, most anti-imperialist militants found it more expedient to revive their slogans against the new world order than to try combining their radical critique of economic globalization with a defense of democratic interventionism patterned after the antifascist stance of the 1930s and 1940s. Moreover, since they could not go so far as supporting Milosevic's "resistance" to Western ag-gression, Western radicals had no other choice than to hastily refashion themselves as champions of national sovereignty. As a result of this choice, anti-imperialist positions acquired a remarkable, albeit unexpected, cohesiveness. Even though the radical wing of the Western Left has hardly been known for its intrinsic affinities with patriotism, in the wake of NATO's campaign, its representatives found themselves defending the privileges of nation-states against international dictates, with respect to social and economic policies as well as human and minority rights.[105]

The future of this emerging polarization between radical friends and liberal foes of national sovereignty will largely depend on whether the rhetoric justifying operation Allied Force proves a binding precedent for Western governments or an isolated exception to the otherwise unmodified doctrine of the international community. In that regard, we have seen that the last few months of the twentieth century offered two contrasting clues. During September 1999, the principles proffered by the victory speeches of NATO leaders after the Serbian retreat from Kosovo did pressure the leading members of the international community into intervening in East Timor, albeit belatedly and begrudgingly, in order to enforce the results of the referendum on independence. Yet, barely one month later, these same principles were conspicuously absent from the reaction of Western governments to the second war launched by the Russian authorities against the secessionist Republic of Chechnya.

Therefore, if it turns out that U.S. and European governments succeed in canceling the liberal hopes and radical fears raised by their proclaimed resolve of the spring of 1999, the two wings of the Western Left may be able to separate their respective assessments of the ills of globalization and flaws of the international community. But if the unexpected return of ideological debates that accompanied NATO's intervention in Kosovo prevents the leading members of the international community from simply ignoring their commitment to oppose massive human rights violations perpetrated by racist regimes—even if the latter happen to be permanent members of the Security Council endowed with a nuclear arsenal—then the incipient antinomy between liberal foes and radical supporters of national sovereignty is bound to persist and deepen. Compared with the period preceding NATO's intervention in Kosovo, this resurgent ideological divide within the Western Left should be welcomed insofar as it helps discredit cultural explanations of post–cold war conflicts and, thus, undermines the self-fulfilling prophecies inherent in the doctrine of the international community. If the principle of national sovereignty remains the primary wedge between liberals and anti-imperialists, however, future disputes between the two wings could prove as wanting, both intellectually and politically, as their quarrels during the cold war. For liberal activists may be increasingly inclined to condone the current mode of economic globalization as a rough but necessary complement to the advancement of democracy and human rights, while anti-imperialist militants may become increasingly involved in the business of downplaying the crimes of nationalist dictators who happen to challenge Western hegemony.

For anyone who sees no reason to choose between endorsing the policies promoted by the IMF and WTO and condoning a strategy of helpless indignation, or even critical engagement, with the perpetrators of ethnic cleansing and genocide, it is certainly tempting to simply discard the terms of the current political debates opposing liberals to anti-imperialists. Such was, for instance, the position taken by the Slovenian philosopher Slavoj Žižek in his article "Against the Double Blackmail," published in both the *Nation* and *Die Zeit* (Germany) during operation Allied Force. For Žižek, the proposed opposition "between enlightened international intervention against ethnic fundamentalists and the heroic last pockets of resistance against the New World Order" was a false one.[106] Since prior to becoming the foe of Western powers Milosevic was the product of their policies — what we have called the doctrine of the international community — Žižek argued that opposing monstrous figures such as the Serbian leader should not amount to supporting the Frankensteins who bred them. Instead of applauding the belated principled proclamations of Clinton and his colleagues — or conversely, of "voicing solidarity with Serbia and condemning NATO bombing" — the Slovenian philosopher called on his leftist brethren to "build *transnational* political movements and institutions strong enough to constrain seriously the unlimited rule of capital and to render visible and politically relevant the fact that the local fundamentalist resistances to the New World Order, from Milosevic to Le Pen and the extreme right in Europe, are part of it."[107]

While these transnational movements and institutions would undeniably be a valuable addition to the current cast of political players on the international scene, Žižek hardly tells us how they would have reacted to the genocide of the Rwandan Tutsis, the ethnic cleansing of the Bosnian Muslims and Albanian Kosovars, or the systematic destruction of East Timor and Chechnya. More precisely, had these movements existed during the 1990s, what conclusions would their spokespeople have drawn from their lucid analysis of the role of Western policies in the atrocities committed by the proponents of Hutu Power, Greater Serbia, Indonesia's "territorial integrity," or Russia's resistance to "international terrorism"? Would they have joined the critics of the international community and asked that the latter's leading members confront the monsters created by their own doctrine? Or would they have claimed, as did the anti-imperialist Left in the spring of 1999, that because of their own record, Western governments were not morally qualified to prevent genocidal regimes from achieving their goals? No matter how determined to resist the "double blackmail" exercised by the friends of global liberalism and foes of the new world order, the lucid transnational movements that Žižek wants the Left to build would have had to opt for one of these two stances.

As such, the intellectuals and activists who seek to alter the terms of the current debate between the two wings of the

Western Left may engage in more fruitful tasks than that of devising a rationale that would simultaneously condemn the likes of Milosevic and deny Western powers the right to oppose them. They could, for instance, reflect on the remarkable similarities existing between the liberals who failed to question the alleged powerlessness of their governments before March 1999 and the radicals who decided to denounce Allied Force as a manifestation of Western imperialism. Though equally offended by the racist nationalisms responsible for the wars in the former Yugoslavia and Rwanda, both groups nonetheless chose to subordinate their revulsion for ethnic cleansing and genocide to their stake in the public image of their own governments. Indeed, what impelled a majority of liberals to believe that their leaders were powerless to prevent the resurgence of ancient ethnic enmities was their more or less conscious fear that reckoning with the cynicism of Western governments might shatter the hopes that they themselves had invested in an international community dominated by liberal democracies. Likewise, what decided most exponents of the anti-imperialist Left to condemn NATO's war against Serbia was their conviction that supporting a military intervention unilaterally decided on by the U.S. administration and its allies would undermine the consistency of their radical opposition to the promoters of the new global economy. In short, radicals who objected to operation Allied Force made it their priority to oppose any action undertaken by governments representing imperialism, whereas the chief concern of liberals who condoned the international community's doctrine was that governments representing the liberal rule of law would not be unredeemably discredited.

If the pitfalls of the resurging ideological dispute between liberals and anti-imperialists are to be avoided, the first task at hand may be to reassess the relationship between governmental and nongovernmental politics, and in particular, do away with the idea that the ultimate goal of political activism consists of being governed by the authentic representatives of one's own values and ideals. By definition, the purpose of a government is to govern, that is, to maximize its influence, both on its constituents and vis-à-vis other governing bodies, at a minimal cost. Insofar as nongovernmental activists intend to remain what they are—rather than embrace the alternative positions either of progovernmental apologists, antigovernmental militants, or apolitical humanitarians—their sole purpose should be to raise the cost of those governmental policies that they consider objectionable. In other words, it is only by recognizing that governments are not meant to represent them that nongovernmental activists will be able to 135 give precedence to the prevention of what they deem intolerable over their stake in either redeeming or condemning the agencies that have the power to prevent it.

Notes

1 Cited in Mark Danner, "Clinton, the UN, and the Bosnian Disaster,"
   New York Review of Books, 7 December 1997.

2 Cited in Roger Cohen, *Hearts Grown Brutal: Sagas of Sarajevo* (New
   York: Random House, 1998), 175.

3 Cited in Danner, "Clinton."

4 Ibid.

5 Bill Clinton cited in Cohen, *Hearts Grown Brutal*, 398.

6 As will be discussed later, Kosovo is the region where Milosevic started
   the process that set the former Yugoslavia aflame. In 1990, three years
   after the Serbian leader first presented himself as the protector of
   Kosovo's Serbs, he removed the autonomous status of the province
   and subsequently submitted the Albanian majority to what can be
   described as a regime of apartheid. Contrary to the old South African rulers, however, Milosevic and his allies only saw this regime as a
   means to a further end. Their ultimate goal was to reverse a secular
   trend in Kosovo's demography and "return" the region to the Serbs.
   They thus envisioned fostering Serbian settlements in Kosovo, but
   also partially "cleansing" the province of its Albanian population,
   either through active mass deportation or just because the dismal political and economic situation of the Albanians would persuade them
   to seek refuge in neighboring countries. Still, Milosevic was aware of
   the contradiction between Kosovo's symbolic importance in the Serbian nationalist agenda and the Serbs' persistent reluctance to actually live there. Until 1998, he refrained from implementing the sec-

ond phase of his plan. Despite his inflammatory rhetoric, the Serbian leader did not actively promote the creation of Serbian colonies in Kosovo, save for the relocation of a few thousand refugees from the Krajina region after the Croat offensive of 1995. Moreover, the presence of U.S. soldiers near the Macedonian border dissuaded him from applying the practice of systematic ethnic cleansing to Kosovo. Therefore, between 1990 and 1997, Albanian Kosovars were spared the fate of the Bosnian Muslims. Yet during that same period, Western governments did little more than deplore the Serbian version of "separate development." Claiming that stability was a prerequisite for a fair settlement, they succeeded in encouraging Milosevic's arrogance — thereby enhancing his victims' rage — and eventually obtained the exact opposite of their purported goal: namely, a full-scale war.

7   Whether still overtly marxist or provisionally converted to Keynes, the anti-imperialist Left has survived the collapse of the Communist bloc. It continues to deserve its name insofar as challenging the social and cultural hegemony of Western capitalism remains its raison d'être. Anti-imperialist activists, however, are less preoccupied than before with the prospect of revolution and the discovery of a proletariat capable of saving socialism from its bureaucratic demons. Instead, what they currently seek is to reconcile environmentalist, antiracist, feminist, and gay and lesbian militants with the proponents of more traditional struggles against class exploitation and neocolonial domination. Supported, in the United States and Europe, by publications such as the *Nation, Le Monde diplomatique, Die Tageszeitung,* or *Il Manifesto* — as well as by intellectuals such as Noam Chomsky, Pierre Bourdieu, or Edward Said — the purpose of this hypothetical reconciliation is to build a transnational movement of resistance against the ongoing process of capitalist globalization and its main promoters, namely, the U.S. government, International Monetary Fund, and World Trade Organization (wto). Among the first victories of this budding "neo-anti-imperialist" movement was its successful lobbying effort against the Multilateral Agreement on Investment, sponsored by the Organization for Economic Cooperation and Development in 1998, according to which sovereign states would have all but renounced the privilege of interfering with foreign investments on their territory. Then, in November 1999, came the

spectacular disruption of the WTO in Seattle, which not only put the movement in the public eye but also made its members and Western governments aware of the renewed appeal of anticapitalist sentiments.

8   Christopher Hitchens, "Minority Report," *Nation*, 20 November 1995.

9   Loath to condone NATO's actions, Hitchens accused Western governments of doing too little too late and suspected them of merely paving the way for a Dayton-like agreement with Milosevic that would lead to the partition of Kosovo. Nevertheless, he mostly used his column to take his *Nation* colleagues to task for favoring a "diplomatic" resolution to the conflict that would amount to letting Milosevic prevail.

10 Editorial, "Stop the War Now," *Nation*, 24 May 1999, 3.

11 On the North Atlantic alliance, see Stephen F. Cohen, " 'Degrading' America," *Nation*, 24 May 1999, 6 ("In truth, US political and military leaders now care little about the morality [or legality] of their actions in Yugoslavia, only the 'credibility of NATO' "). On undermining the UN, see editorial, "Dark Victory," *Nation*, 28 June 1999. ("It was at Rambouillet that NATO first revealed what turned out to be its goal throughout the war: to assert unilaterally military authority over Serbia while systematically excluding the UN").

12 A similar analysis can be made about European leftist publications. In the French monthly *Le Monde diplomatique*, for instance, it was the same journalist, Serge Halimi, who expressed the periodical's disgust for UN and Western inaction in July 1995, and for NATO's intervention in the spring of 1999. The European anti-imperialist Left also suggested that the Clinton administration had additional motives for launching operation Allied Force, such as keeping its European allies under U.S. tutelage, driving a wedge between Russia and the rest of Europe, and securing access for the United States to the oil of the Caspian Sea.

13 From 1990 to 1998, U.S. as well as other Western officials condoned the policy of Rugova because the Kosovar leader was urging his Albanian constituency to resist Serbian oppression with civil disobedience rather than military confrontation. Yet, while praising Rugova's moderation, Western governments persistently undermined his position. Although allegedly in favor of Kosovo's provincial autonomy, they never pressured Milosevic into restoring the civil rights of the

Albanian community. In particular, the Dayton agreements did not set the reinstatement of Kosovo's autonomy as a necessary condition either for lifting economic sanctions on Milosevic's regime or granting diplomatic recognition to Yugoslavia. To the contrary, Western officials went out of their way to placate the Serbian leader by publicizing their irrevocable opposition to Kosovo's independence. After enduring an eight-year stalemate, therefore, an increasing number of Albanians lost faith in Rugova's strategy, investing their hopes in the rapidly growing KLA instead.

14　How Milosevic managed to undermine Western claims to impartiality can be recounted as follows. First, on February 28, 1998, only days after Gelbard called the KLA a terrorist organization, Serbian troops launched their first military campaign in the Drenica region of central Kosovo, destroying scores of villages and perpetrating a number of massacres—such as in Likoshani and Prekaz—under the pretext of fighting Albanian terrorism. Second, in the summer of 1998, ignoring the supposedly strong final warnings issued by Western powers, Belgrade stepped up its campaign: thus, by September, about 300 Albanian villages had been destroyed and 300,000 people driven from their homes. Third, in December 1998, Milosevic reneged on the agreement he had signed two months earlier, according to which he was to suspend all military action in Kosovo, withdraw most of his special troops, and allow Organization for Security and Cooperation in Europe (OSCE) observers to "verify" the peace. Not only did the Serbian leader initiate a new offensive in northeastern Kosovo but he also amassed at least 15,000 troops near the border of the province, ostensibly in preparation for a massive spring campaign. Finally, on January 15, 1999, Serbian military and/or paramilitary troops committed yet another massacre, killing forty-five people in the village of Raçak. When the head of the OSCE mission called this action a crime against humanity, Milosevic immediately asked for his removal.

15　On pacifist outcries, see Tom Hayden, "The Liberals' Folly," *Nation*, 24 May 1999, 5. Not to sound too isolationist, Hayden also stressed that the Clinton administration was spending more on one month of war in the Balkans "than on the entire budget for Central American victims of Hurricane Mitch." On righteous denunciations, as Ian Williams, one of the two dissenting voices in the *Nation*, replied to his colleagues, this stance implied that only governments with pure intentions would be morally qualified to oppose genocide or systematic ethnic cleansing.

16 There is, of course, an easy answer to this purportedly rhetorical question, namely, that the precedent created by NATO's intervention in Kosovo—especially in the context of the hopes raised by Augusto Pinochet's arrest and Milosevic's indictments for crimes against humanity—can provide human rights activists with a better chance to weigh in on the policies of Western democracies vis-à-vis Turkey, Israel, or China. Conversely, would the causes of the Kurds, Palestinians, and Tibetans be better served by NATO turning a blind eye to the continued oppression and—at best—gradual deportation of the Kosovars? Though he did not quite say why, the Palestinian American scholar Edward Said seemed to think so. In an article published by the Egyptian newspaper *Al Ahram* in the spring of 1999, Said all but agreed with the Serbian sociologist Aleksa Djilas—the author, in April 1998, of an essay titled "Whatever Israel Does to the Palestinians, We Serbs Can Do to the Albanians"—that having supported Israeli ethnic cleansers in 1948, the United States was morally obliged to tolerate Milosevic's atrocities. In contrast, Ariel Sharon, the right-wing Israeli politician, publicly disapproved of Allied Force on the basis that the discourse justifying it would eventually prove detrimental to Israel's interests.

141

17 According to the Dayton Peace Agreement the Implementation Force (IFOR)—the first name given to NATO troops in Bosnia—also had the right to bivouac in Yugoslavia.

18 Compared to the previous documents submitted to the parties by Western diplomats—in particular, the 1998 "Hill plan," named after the U.S. ambassador to Macedonia, Christopher Hill—the final draft of the Rambouillet Agreement included a crucial new clause. The latter stated that "three years after the entry into force of this Agreement, an international meeting shall be convened to determine a mechanism for a final settlement for Kosovo, on the basis of the will of the people." It was the first time that the representatives of the international community were presenting Kosovo's eventual independence as an option. On the Rambouillet negotiations, see the preface to Noel Malcolm, *Kosovo: A Short History* (New York: Harper Perennial, 1999);

and Paul Garde, "Kosovo: Missile intelligent et chausse-pied rouillé," *Politique Internationale* 84 (summer 1999): 26–29.

19 Quote from "Stop the War Now," *Nation*, 24 May 1999, 4. That no Kosovar refugee would have come back under these circumstances — not to mention that no Albanian delegation would have ever signed this alternative agreement — did not seem to bother the *Nation* editors. But we should remember that according to anti-imperialist commentators, the massive deportation of the Albanian population was the consequence of operation Allied Force, not a longstanding Serbian plan to "solve" the "demographic problem" in Kosovo once and for all. Therefore, the editors of the *Nation* considered that since Western governments held a larger share of responsibility for the tragic lot of the Kosovars than the ethnic cleansers themselves, it was their duty to accommodate the refugees in the West rather than imposing them on the Serbs.

20 Because progressive venues such as the *Nation* reacted to the new discourse of the Clinton administration by taking over the old one — despite the fact that they used to criticize it — it was obviously not their place to underscore the contradiction between the successive positions of the U.S. government. Yet, remarkably enough, the leftist detractors of Allied Force were not the only ones to minimize the change of discourse — or at least the importance of such a change — that accompanied Clinton's decision to bomb Serbia. Though initially relieved that Western powers had finally decided to confront Milosevic, internationalist liberals and human rights advocates, who had been the staunchest critics of Western inaction in the former Yugoslavia, did not make much of the sudden disappearance of the ancient enmity explanation that they themselves had denounced in vain for almost a decade. Rather than celebrating the fact that ethnic cleansing was finally officially identified as the implementation of a political project, and not the flaring up of a cultural disease, these anti-"appeasement" activists mostly lamented about the way in which this belated reassessment of the Yugoslav wars was actualized. For instance, essayists like Philip Gourevitch (in the *New Yorker*) and Mark Danner (in the *New York Review of Books*) — who had eloquently denounced the tribalization of post–cold war conflicts by U.S. officials, respectively, in Bosnia and Rwanda — complained that by limiting its intervention

to an air campaign, NATO was giving precedence to the safety of its soldiers over that of Kosovar civilians. They thus contended that the means used by NATO to accomplish its objectives threatened to annul the doctrinal change expressed in the alliance's decision to intervene.

21 True to form, the "world policemen" argument was used by Secretary of Defense William Cohen—acting more as the Pentagon's spokesperson than that of the Clinton administration—on September 8, 1999. Meanwhile, National Security adviser Berger, faithful to his own words of caution in the aftermath of operation Allied Force, insisted on the fact that there was no institution comparable to NATO in Asia. Berger therefore concluded that any attempt to bypass the UN Security Council would be deeply resented by Asian nations.

22 On "two wrongs don't make a right," see Cohen, " 'Degrading' America," *Nation*, 24 May 1999, 6. The two wrongs, equally reprehensible in Cohen's eyes, were Milosevic's ethnic cleansing campaign and NATO's air war.

23 Because of their own record in Chechnya and Tibet, Russian and Chinese authorities have been particularly keen to prevent the UN Security Council from taking too strong a stance against any political regime whose only crime consists of staving off separatism by persecuting ethnic or national minorities. Mixing their old anti-imperialist rhetoric with a restrictive interpretation of international law, the former leaders of the Communist bloc have relentlessly professed that a sovereign state, regardless of the human rights violations committed by its representatives, must be allowed to conduct its domestic affairs without interference from foreign powers.

24 Already during the air strikes, most of the articles that the *Nation* devoted to Kosovo emphasized that condemning Allied Force did not amount to condoning Belgrade's atrocities. Still, until Milosevic's capitulation enabled the refugees to come back to their burned out homes, these same articles could claim that NATO's intervention had made things worse: not only had the operation been incapable of preventing Serbian forces from expelling nearly a million Albanians but, according to the *Nation*, Serbian troops and militias would not have cleansed Kosovo of its Albanian population had Western powers refrained from resorting to force. Of course, in order to make this last assertion—and thus denounce as two equally repellent crimes the

slaughter and massive deportation of the Kosovars and the bombing of Serbia—the *Nation* had to ignore the fact that while the Rambouillet negotiations were taking place, Milosevic had gathered about 40,000 troops on the northern border of Kosovo. On the events leading to the launching of Allied force, see the preface to Noel Malcolm, *Kosovo: A Short History* (New York: Harper Perennial, 1999); and Florence Hartman, *Milosevic: La diagonale du fou* (Paris: Denoël, 1999), 400–401.

25 On August 30, 1999, 79 percent of East Timorese voted against the limited autonomy status proposed to them by the Indonesian government of President B. J. Habibie, thereby expressing their unwavering desire to obtain full independence. While the referendum was organized by the UN mission in East Timor the secretary general of the United Nations agreed to let Indonesian forces assume responsibility for the population's safety in the wake of the vote. As in Rwanda five years earlier, Kofi Annan took the chance of disregarding a report written by his own administration. In this case, it revealed that anti-independence militias, under the guidance of Indonesian security forces, were planning to respond to an unfavorable result at the polls with a campaign of systematic murders—eradication of the pro-independence elite—destruction of the major cities, and deportation of large portions of the population to West Timor.

26 Though they never formally recognized the subsequent annexation of East Timor in 1976 as Indonesia's "twenty-seventh province," U.S. administrations, from Gerald Ford and Jimmy Carter to Clinton's, all but condoned the brutal occupation, and thus, the killing of 200,000 East Timorese by the Indonesian armed forces. After Henry Kissinger famously declared that he understood Indonesia's decision to invade a territory whose right to self-determination had just been recognized by the UN, all his successors at the State Department worked hard at keeping Suharto's crimes from the scrutiny of the Security Council, while the Pentagon continued to train the special forces responsible for them.

27 Editorial, "East Timor's Agony," *Nation*, 20 September 1999, 3.

28 Opposition to the North American Free Trade Agreement (NAFTA) in the United States and the Maastricht Treaty establishing the European Union in Europe already brought together the extreme and iso-

lationist Right, on the one hand—Pat Buchanan, Jean-Marie Le Pen, Ross Perot, Euro-skeptic Tories in Britain and Gaullists in France, and the like—and the radical and populist Left, on the other hand— Communists, Trotskyites, a majority of unions, and what we have dubbed the anti-imperialist Left. Of course, rightist and leftist detractors of NAFTA and the EU raised very different arguments against the two treaties: the former denounced them for debilitating national sovereignty, whereas the latter faulted them for liberalizing trade and capital flows at the expense of working conditions. Yet, however ad hoc, this coalition already pointed to a potential ideological realignment whereby nationalist militants would emphasize the social dimension of their opposition to multinational treaties, while leftist activists would hail the nation-state as the main site of democratic resistance to global capitalism.

29   As we will see later, some of the harshest critics of Western policies throughout the Bosnian War and during the Rwandan genocide were liberal essayists and journalists—writing for publications such as the *New Yorker, New York Review of Books,* and *New Republic* in the United States, and *Esprit* in France—who had basically endorsed the proposition that post–cold war liberalism involved preventing states from regulating economic forces as well as stifling human rights and civil liberties. Having done what they saw as their part of the deal, namely, renouncing their former faith in the welfare state in favor of a mix of free trade and empathy elusively dubbed the "third way," they were understandably outraged that all they received in return from Western governments was a policy of appeasement worthy of the 1930s and the deliberate cover-up of a genocide.

30   In a chilling article titled "Left-Right Bedfellows" (*Nation,* 28 June 1999), Benjamin Schwarz actually celebrated the prospect of a budding coalition between the anti-imperialist Left and isolationist Right. In his own words, "Most thoughtful leftists have long known that when it comes to a serious critique of U.S. foreign policy, they have far more in common with elements of the right than they do with the Cold War liberals and their globalist progeny currently running U.S. diplomacy. . . . NATO's war against Serbia has given anti-imperialist progressives and conservatives . . . their best chance to mobilize ordi-

nary Americans—who have always maintained a healthy skepticism toward the foreign policies advocated by the globalist elite that dominates both political parties—in an effort to change fundamental U.S. global strategy." Nevertheless, one can still assume—or at least hope—that most anti-imperialist activists would not be so thrilled to join hands with the populist followings of Buchanan, Le Pen, and other glorious exponents of the patriotic resistance to globalization.

31   The first Chechen war was initiated by the Yeltsin regime in December 1994—some three years after Chechen President Dzhokhar Dudayev unilaterally declared independence—and ended in the summer of 1996 with Russian troops pulling out, after Chechen forces managed to reconquer most of Grozny, Chechnya's capital. The peace treaty signed by the two parties stipulated that the final status of Chechnya would be decided through negotiations in 2001.

32   For good measure, the Bush administration also worked hard at portraying Hussein as a new Hitler, even if having supported the Iraqi regime throughout its war against Iran, between 1981 and 1988, U.S. officials tended to make more of imaginary atrocities allegedly committed by Iraqi troops in Kuwait than the real genocidal war that Hussein had waged against the Iraqi Kurds during the 1980s—and that every Western leader had all but condoned.

33   To the contrary, U.S. Commander in Chief General Norman Schwarzkopf went as far as authorizing the Iraqi armed forces to use their helicopters against the rebels. For Bush's call to the Iraqi people, see Andrew and Patrick Cockburn, *Out of the Ashes: The Resurrection of Saddem Hussein* (New York: Harper Collins, 1999), 12–13.

34   In their book, *Out of the Ashes: The Resurrection of Saddam Hussein*, Andrew and Patrick Cockburn amply demonstrate that Bush's address of February 15, 1991, was very much at odds with the general policy of his administration, which consisted of fomenting—or at least hoping for—a military coup against Hussein rather than supporting a democratic revolution in Iraq. Among other examples, the two authors tell the story of Laith Kubba, a member of the Iraqi opposition, who in the immediate wake of Hussein's aggression toward Kuwait, suggested to a State Department official "that the United States use the invasion crisis to advance the cause of democracy in Iraq. 'Who told you we want democracy in Iraq?' answered the official.

... 'It would offend our friends the Saudis' " (49). The coauthors also report that when Peter Galbraith, who was then staff director for the Senate Foreign Relations Committee, publicly supported the Kurdish rebellion, he drew the following reprimand from Richard Haass, director for Middle East affairs at the National Security Council: " 'You don't understand,' fumed the powerful White House official. 'Our policy is to get rid of Saddam, not his regime' " (37).

35 That the international tribunals for the former Yugoslavia and Rwanda managed to assert their independence from Western governments, and thus accomplish precisely what the latter did not want them to do, should be credited to the courage and persistence of their first two chief prosecutors, Richard Goldstone and Louise Arbour. Conversely, the fact that Western leaders applauded Milosevic's indictment by the international tribunal for the former Yugoslavia during NATO's intervention in Kosovo — when it helped justify their war effort — should not let anyone forget that prior to the launching of operation Allied Force, they deliberately withheld information that would have aided Arbour in building her case against Milosevic.

147

36 Regarding the war in the former Yugoslavia, scholarly critics of the intractable Balkan enmity theory included, among others, the historians Noel Malcolm and Martha Vickers, the linguist Paul Garde, the political scientists Norman Cigar and Pierre Hassner, and the sociologists Stjepan Mestrovic and Thomas Cushman. In terms of Rwanda, detractors of the tribalization of the genocide included, among others, the historians Alison Des Forges, Claudine Vidal, Jean-Pierre Chrétien, and Gérard Prunier, the geographer Dominique Franche, and the legal scholar Françoise Bouchet-Saulnier.

37 While some relief organizations applauded the identification of Western governments with their own humanitarian concerns, others, led by Doctors without Borders, claimed that humanitarianism was neither the proper response to genocide and ethnic cleansing nor even an appropriate motivation for governmental policies. According to this Paris-based organization, the humanitarian rhetoric eagerly displayed by Western officials was less the sign of a rapprochement between governments and NGOs than a cynical attempt, on the part of the former, to conceal their lack of resolve through the co-optation of the latter's concerns.

38 Roy Gutman, David Rieff, Roger Cohen, Chuck Sudetic, Jean Hatz-
    feld, Florence Hartmann, David Rohde, and Mark Danner were
    among the most vocal critics of the impartiality of the international
    community in Bosnia; Colette Braeckman, Rony Brauman, Alain
    Destexhe—who like Brauman, used to work with Doctors without
    Borders—and Philip Gourevitch stigmatized Western policies dur-
    ing the Rwandan genocide.

39 For instance, beyond their strictly humanitarian function, Doctors
    without Borders made it their constant mission to convey that gov-
    ernments, armies, and rebel guerrillas of all ideological persuasions
    should be exposed for the suffering they inflicted on civilian popula-
    tions. As for Amnesty International and Human Rights Watch, the
    essence of their work has always been to report on all human rights
    violations, regardless of the political orientation of the regimes that
    committed them.

40 Serbs were indeed persecuted and massacred in the independent Cro-
    atian state of Ante Pavelic (1941–1945). Yet the crimes of the Ustashas
    expressed the political nature of Pavelic's regime—an ally and emu-
    lator of the Nazis, as was the Serbian regime of General Milan Nedic—
    rather than any ingrained sentiments among the Croatian people.
    Even if the partisan movement gathered more Serbs at first, by 1943,
    Croats and Serbs were evenly represented in Tito's resistance move-
    ment against the German invaders as well as the collaborationist re-
    gimes of Pavelic and Nedic.

41 In 1389, Prince Lazar was defeated, and later beheaded, by the army
    of Sultan Murad in a place called Kosovo Polje. In the Serbian nation-
    alist mythology of the late nineteenth and early twentieth centuries,
    this battle symbolized the demise of the Serbian empire and the en-
    slavement of the Serbian people by the Turks. Therefore, ridding what
    used to be Serbian, Orthodox soil of its "Turkish," Muslim popula-
    tion—in Kosovo and Bosnia—has been one of the central objectives
    of the radical proponents of a Greater Serbia.

42 The distinction between Tutsis and Hutus precedes the colonial pe-
    riod. Yet, until the twentieth century, it was never understood as an
    ethnic difference: Tutsis and Hutus spoke the same language, occu-
    pied the same territory, and shared the same religion and myths. The
    latter even asserted that they were the children of a common ancestor.

According to the geographer Dominique Franche, Hutu or Tutsi was merely one among several "categories"—*bwoko* in Kinyarwanda—that defined the social identity of an individual, along with his or her region of origin, lineage, and profession. Politically, it is true that the *mwami*—usually translated as king—was of Tutsi lineage; but his authority—which did not extend to the north of the country, where some of the most powerful families were Hutu—was not based on the fact that he was a Tutsi. The colonizers, however, projected their own racial theories onto the Rwandans: without the shadow of a proof, they stated that the tall, European-looking Tutsis had come from Abyssinia—the so-called Hamitic theory—and colonized the local Hutus. Relying on this mythology, the German and later Belgian colonial administrations treated the Tutsis as the governing elite. They reserved access to the better schools to Tutsi children, and then used the better-educated Tutsis as intermediaries between themselves and the rest of the population. Understandably, this self-serving application of modern racial theory gave birth to a modern form of racism between the two communities. The ethnic tension created by the colonizers and nurtured by the brutal ways of the empowered Tutsi aristocracy culminated at the end of the colonial period. Eager to deflect the mounting protest against its colonial rule, the Belgian administration suddenly embraced the cause of the oppressed Hutu majority—about 85 percent of the population—and even encouraged them to rebel against the tyranny of the Tutsis. The actual independence of Rwanda was thus preceded by a violent "Hutu revolution" that rid the country of its much resented aristocracy but also defined the political life of postcolonial Rwanda in ill-fated ethnic terms.

43 Currently the governing party in Rwanda, until 1994, the RPF was a rebel organization based in Uganda and largely, though not exclusively, made up of children of Tutsi exiles. Tutsis started fleeing Rwanda in 1959, after 20,000 of them were killed in the massacre known as the Rwandan All-Saints Day (Toussaint Rwandaise). They continued to leave through the early 1960s in order to escape the racist and violent policies of the ruling Hutu Party (Parmehutu).

44 Paradoxically, as Tim Judah showed in his book, *The Serbs: History, Myth, and the Destruction of Yugoslavia* (New Haven, Conn.: Yale University Press, 1997), the renewal of Serbian nationalism in the mid-

1980s did not originate in overtly reactionary circles or among cynical apparatchiks but in a group of intellectuals such as Mihailo Markovic and Dobrica Cosic, who in the 1960s and 1970s, had been known as dissidents with liberal leanings and as civil rights activists. Markovic had been the main organizer of the semiclandestine Free University, and Cosic the chief spokesperson for the Committee for the Freedom of Speech (see 156–60).

45 Milosevic first presented himself as the protector of the Serbs in April 1987: his proclamation had a particularly dramatic impact because it took place in Kosovo Polje, the site of the famous 1389 battle. In 1987, Kosovo, though 90 percent Albanian, was an autonomous province within Serbia. Yet there were increasing tensions between the political representatives of the Albanian majority, who were demanding

that Kosovo receive the status of a sovereign republic, and the leaders of the Serbian minority, who were spreading unsubstantiated rumors according to which the Albanian majority was in the process of expelling the Serbs from Kosovo, the very cradle of their civilization. Although Serbs were already a minority in Kosovo three centuries ago, the demographic reconquest of the province has been the central tenet of Serbian nationalism for about a hundred years. Between the two world wars, the governments of King Alexander attempted, albeit unsuccessfully, both to send Serb settlers to Kosovo and expel Albanians—who were already the majority—from their homeland. Tito, in contrast, tried, not too successfully either, both to satisfy Serbian demands by keeping Kosovo within Serbia and win over the Albanian population by granting them an increasing degree of autonomy. The immediate post-Tito era corresponded to a surge of Albanian nationalism: Kosovar politicians asked at once for an upgrade of Kosovo's status, from autonomous province to full-fledged republic, and an evolution of Yugoslavia's constitution, from a federation to a confederation of independent states. In contrast, Milosevic's rise to power brought back King Alexander's plan of "returning" Kosovo to the Serbs.

46 Under the constitution of 1974, the Yugoslav federation included six republics—Serbia, Montenegro, Croatia, Bosnia-Hercegovina, Slovenia, and Macedonia—and two autonomous provinces within Serbia—Vojvodina and Kosovo. Except for the right to secede, the two

autonomous provinces had practically the same rights as the six republics. In particular, each of these eight entities had one vote in the "collegial presidency" of the federation. Thus, to prevent the supporters of a confederation—that is, the representatives of Slovenia, Croatia, Bosnia, Macedonia, and Kosovo—from taking control of the collegial presidency, Milosevic resorted to the following maneuver: he suspended Vojvodina and Kosovo's autonomous governments without suppressing the autonomy of the two provinces. Consequently, their votes in the collegial presidency reverted back to Serbia. The Serbian government and its Montenegran ally controlled four out of eight votes in the collegial presidency, thanks to this manipulation, which meant that they could block any motion to change the constitution.

47   In July 1990, once the provincial assembly and government were dis- **151** solved, the Serbian leadership took advantage of the state of emergency it had imposed to enforce far more radical measures: ethnic Albanians were expelled from state-owned universities and schools, Albanian judges and civil servants were removed from office, Albanian doctors were fired from public hospitals, Albanian journalists were purged from the official media, and so on.

48   One of the main features of the new regime was that northern Hutus replaced southern Hutus at the head of the state. Historians of Rwanda such as Catharine Newbury, Clandine Vidal, and Jean-Pierre Chrétien have shown that in precolonial times, the opposition between the powerful lineages of the north—both Hutu and Tutsi—and their counterparts in the south—the mwami and his vassals' lineages—was as politically meaningful as the distinction between Hutus and Tutsis.

49   Instrumental in the organization of the genocide, this measure also proves that there is no ethnic difference between the Hutus and Tutsis. For if the "tall, European-looking" Tutsis were so easily recognizable, there would be no need to verify their ethnicity on their passports. Nazi anti-Semitism harbored the same paradox: on the one hand, Jews were supposedly morphologically distinct from Aryans; on the other hand, they somehow managed to make themselves indistinguishable from the rest of the population.

50   Indeed, both Mitterrand and his successor continued to support the regimes of Mobutu Sese Seke in Zaire, Gnassingbé Eyadema in Togo,

Paul Biya in Cameroon, Omar Bongo in Gabon, and Idriss Deby in Chad, to name only a few.

51 In September 1990, Habyarimana appointed a national commission whose purpose was to "identify what the concept of democracy means to the Rwandan majority" (cited in Filip Reyntjens, *L'Afrique des Grands Lacs en crise* [Paris: Karthala, 1994], 91).

52 In the early 1980s, RPF soldiers had fought in the Ugandan civil war, with the National Resistance Army of Yoweri Museveni, and their help had been crucial to Museveni's rise to power.

53 The main center of power in Rwanda, the *Akazu* ("little house"), included the families of both Habyarimana and his wife. It was dominated by the president's in-laws, who were among the most radical proponents of Hutu hegemony.

54 Regarding the support granted to Habyarimana, until 1994, the French ambassador, in contrast with his Belgian, Canadian, and Swiss colleagues, either downplayed or even denied the reports of human rights violations in Rwanda. As for the Hutu Power networks, they gathered the major adversaries of the peace process, including journalists, intellectuals, army officers, and politicians. Among the latter were high officials from the president's MRND and the leaders of an openly racist party, the CDR (Coalition pour la Défense de la République). Furthermore, the Hutu Power networks even managed to infiltrate opposition parties whose leaders favored the Arusha agreements.

55 Regarding the murderous propaganda, the "Ten Commandments of the Hutu," published in 1990, asked Hutus to stop all dealings, private as well as professional, with the Tutsis, while the semiofficial Radio Télévision Mille Collines—funded mostly by the Akazu—started calling for the extermination of all Tutsis in the summer of 1993. As for the death squads, the Interahamwe and Impuzamugambi, respectively the militias of the MRND and CDR, committed their first massacres in 1991. Mostly trained by French instructors, the Interahamwe militia took a major part in the genocide of 1994.

56 The Rwandan president was killed on his way back from Dar es-Salaam, Tanzania, where he had finally agreed to endorse a coalition government led by a member of the democratic opposition and includ-

ing two RPF ministers. His plane was shot down just before landing in Kigali, and his assassins were never clearly identified.

57   Meanwhile, the Yugoslav army—which had sided with the Serbian government in the late 1980s and subsequently become a purely Serbian institution—and Rwandan armed forces were officially required to maintain the authority of their respective states in a time of "ethnic" unrest. Practically, however, the main tasks of these regular armies consisted of sealing off the targeted areas before the killings— letting the militias in but preventing the civilians from getting out— and then reestablishing "order" after the killings.

58   About the successive conflicts in Kosovo, Croatia, and Bosnia, James Baker—then Bush's secretary of state—had famously declared that he had no dog in those fights.

59   In particular, U.S. diplomats were instrumental in ending the war   **153** between Bosnian Croats and Bosnian Muslims, in establishing the Bosnian-Croat Federation in March 1994, and in letting the Croatian and, to a lesser extent, the Bosnian armies acquire some weapons, despite the arms embargo.

60   In May 1994, the Degni-Ségui report, sponsored by the UN Human Rights Commission, concluded that a genocide was indeed taking place in Rwanda. On June 10, 1994, however, a spokesperson for the White House still declared that while genocidal acts had probably been perpetrated, the term *genocide* did not apply to all the crimes committed in Rwanda. It was only on July 1, 1994, when more than a half million people had already been murdered, that the U.S. government realized that such a "logic" was untenable. The Clinton administration agreed to an official inquiry commissioned by the UN Security Council and purported to investigate "possible acts of genocide on the territory of Rwanda" (Security Council, Resolution 935).

61   The French authorities recognized the so-called interim government that succeeded Habyarimana, received its representatives in Paris three weeks after the beginning of the genocide, and in spite of the French government's denial, delivered weapons to the Rwandan Armed Forces until July 1994.

62   Until the summer of 1992, Mitterrand refused to speak of a Serbian aggression, despite the destruction of Vukovar, the siege of Sarajevo,

the occupation of Slavonia and the Croatian Krajina, and the ethnic cleansing of half of Bosnia. Then, as long as he remained in power, he repeatedly opposed any military action against the Bosnian Serb militias, arguing that it would only "add more war to war" (*"il ne faut pas ajouter la guerre à la guerre"*), his motto until 1995. Moreover, he never ceased to claim that Germany's early recognition of Croatia and Slovenia had been the main cause of the Yugoslav wars (Germany recognized Slovenia and Croatia on December 23, 1991, three weeks before the other countries of the European Community, but more than a month after the Yugoslav army had reduced the city of Vukovar to ashes).

63 Between October 1990 and April 1994, the French authorities provided ample military assistance to the Rwandan Armed Forces (FAR), while their own troops were not only training Rwandan soldiers but also actively helping them counter the guerrilla operations waged by the RPF. Indeed, beyond their role as instructors, French officers are said to have, minimally, supervised the control of roadblocks and participated in the interrogations of suspects. Moreover, in 1992, French Lieutenant-Colonel Chollet was appointed as special adviser to FAR's chief of staff.

64 As far as being Anglophone, while it is true that the cadres of the RPF learned English during their Ugandan exile, this argument nonetheless reveals the persistence of the colonial imagination: in Rwanda, except for a small minority, both Hutus and Tutsis merely speak Kinyarwanda.

65 A similar analysis could be made for British Prime Minister John Major, who largely shared the French view on the Yugoslav situation and the U.S. position on Rwanda.

66 One could even argue that the perpetual bickering that went on between the leading members of the international community served the consistency of their common policy quite well insofar as it allowed each government or international institution to blame the others for the pusillanimity of their collective action.

67 Even the U.S. Congress was advocating the "lift and strike" option, which would have provided weapons for the Bosnian army and authorized NATO planes to bomb Mladic's positions.

68 In fact, French troops intervened twice during the Rwandan conflict.

Their first operation, called Amaryllis, was secret and did not have a UN mandate. Its purposes were to get French nationals out of the country, but also—when it became clear that the perpetrators of the genocide were losing the war—to evacuate Habyarimana's family and other Hutu dignitaries who had worked closely with their French protectors.

69 Radio Télévision Mille Collines, the radio station that had called for the extermination of the Tutsis since 1993, continued to broadcast its heinous messages from the Turquoise security zone until mid-July 1994.

70 The September 1991 conference on Yugoslavia, organized by the European Community and presided over by Lord Peter Carrington, soon became a joint endeavor, sponsored by the UN as well. Its successive copresidents were Lord Carrington, Lord David Owen, and Carl Bildt on the European Community side, and Cyrus Vance and Thorvald Stoltenberg for the UN.

71 The "rehearsal" massacres began in 1991, when 1,200 Bagogwe—a small subgroup of Tutsis—were killed in northwest Rwanda by the newly formed militias. Then, in 1992, several hundred Tutsis as well as members of the Hutu opposition to Habyarimana were slaughtered successively in the regions of Bugesera, Kibuye, and Gisenyi. The commissioners of these massacres clearly envisaged them as a test: the point was to see if and how the international community would react. The results were very much to the liking of Habyarimana's entourage, despite the fact that in March 1993, an international commission published an alarming report on human rights violations in Rwanda. Indeed, this disturbing information did not deter the French authorities from actively supporting Habyarimana's regime, while other European countries merely evoked the possibility of sanctions.

In addition, in January 1994, Roméo Dallaire, commander of UNAMIR—the UN contingent that was supposed to supervise the implementation of the Arusha agreements—was informed by an Interahamwe deserter that Habyarimana's entourage was planning to exterminate the Rwandan Tutsis. The informer also gave the locations of the caches where UN troops could find the weapons that were going to be used for the genocide. The UN commander sent a fax to his superiors in New York—as well as a copy to the French, U.S., and Belgian

embassies — warning them about the imminent launching of an extermination campaign and asking permission to seize the weapons. The
UN peacekeeping agency, headed at the time by Kofi Annan, told him
to do nothing about it.

72 As early as October 1991, Karadzic had clearly warned the Bosnian
parliament that his party, the Serbian Democratic Party (SDS), would
interpret a declaration of independence as a casus belli. Based on what
was happening at the time in Croatia, his threat was obviously a serious one. Yet, since a large majority of the Bosnian population favored
independence, the European Commission gave its go ahead to a referendum in February 1992. In order to prevent the escalation of violence, Alija Izetbegovic, the future president of Bosnia-Hercegovina,
asked the UN to send peacekeepers before the official independence
day (March 3, 1992). But Boutros Boutros-Ghali, then secretary general of the UN, flatly refused.

73 The Security Council reduced the number of blue helmets from 2,700
to 450 on April 21, 1994. Two factors motivated this decision: European and U.S. citizens had been evacuated and ten Belgian peacekeepers had been killed by the Rwandan Armed Forces.

74 The only exception was the 1997 report commissioned by the Belgian Senate that exposed the grave flaws of Belgium's policy vis-à-
vis Rwanda in the years and months preceding the genocide. Yet, as
Alison Des Forges explains in the monumental *Leave None to Tell the
Story* (New York: Human Rights Watch, 1999), what even this report
still failed to do was establish the personal responsibility of the Belgian politicians involved.

75 First, as Des Forges reports in *Leave None to Tell the Story*, U.S. and
UN officials decided not to publicize the findings of Robert Gersony, a
consultant for the UN High Committee for Refugees who investigated
the massacres committed by RPF forces during the spring and summer
of 1994. This decision was particularly momentous because Gersony
estimated that as many as 30,000 people might have been killed and
that some of the massacres — most notably in Mukingi and Runda in
southern Rwanda — consisted of arbitrary killings of civilians ordered
by RPF officers. According to Des Forges, the U.S. administration,
eager to compensate for its inaction during the genocide, chose to
conceal Gersony's testimony in order to protect the Rwandan govern-

ment. As for UN officials, their primary apprehension was that new revelations of massacres ignored by UNAMIR would make their organization look even worse. Second, in the winter of 1996–1997, along with Ugandan and Angolan forces, the Rwandan army enabled Laurent Kabila to overthrow the Mobutu regime in the former Zaire. During their military campaign through what is now the Democratic Republic of the Congo, Rwandan troops disbanded the camps of Rwandan Hutu refugees who had fled the advancing RPF in the wake of the genocide. Although the targets of these attacks were the remnants of the Rwandan Armed Forces and Interahamwe militia who were running the camps, in June 1998, the UN Secretary General Investigative Team (SGIT) confirmed that Rwandan and Congolese soldiers were implicated in the indiscriminate slaughter of thousands of refugees. Yet, on July 13, 1998, the UN Security Council decided to shelve the report **157** of the SGIT—or more precisely, to let the Kinshasa and Kigali governments take the appropriate measures—because acting on it would destabilize Rwanda and the Congo (see Amnesty International news release, July 15, 1998).

76   In Burundi, where the structure of the population is roughly the same as in Rwanda—85 percent Hutu and 15 percent Tutsi—the Tutsi "aristocracy" of the colonial period managed to stay in power after the country became independent in 1962. Initially, the ruling party—the Party of Unity and National Progress (Uprona)—of what was then a constitutional monarchy included Hutus as well as Tutsis and its platform ignored ethnic issues. However, as the ethnicist ideology of the Rwandan Parmehutu started to contaminate Burundi, a group of Tutsi officers led by Secretary of Defense Michel Micombero successively managed to take control of the army and establish a one-party republic—through a coup in November 1966. Since then, and except for a brief period of democratization in the early 1990s—between the 1993 election of Melchior Ndadaye, the first Hutu president of the country who was assassinated less than a year after his election, and the coup of Major Pierre Buyoya in 1995—Burundi has remained a military dictatorship caught between the ruling Tutsi junta—even though the official ideology of the regime professes that there is no difference between Hutus and Tutsis—and the Hutu militias of the Party for the Liberation of the Hutu People (Palipehutu), whose ideology

and methods are the same as those of the Interahamwe in Rwanda. On Burundi, see Jean-Pierre Chrétien, *Le défi de l'ethnisme: Rwanda et Burundi, 1990–1996* (Paris: Karthala, 1997), and *L'Afrique des Grands Lacs: Deux mille ans d'histoire* (Paris: Aubier, 2000).

77 The International War Crimes Tribunal for the former Yugoslavia is located in The Hague and was instituted in February 1993, while the International War Crimes Tribunal for Rwanda is in Arusha and was created in November 1994.

78 As for arresting indicted war criminals, Karadzic and Mladic, in particular, were still free in the winter of 2000. In terms of new indictments, as we have seen earlier, until they changed their own approach in 1999, Western governments actively hindered the efforts that Louise Arbour, the second chief prosecutor of the International War Crimes Tribunal for the former Yugoslavia, deployed to indict Milosevic.

158

79 In 1997, French Defense Minister Alain Richard famously declared that he did not want French officers exposed to the "show-business justice" (*"justice spectacle"*) of the International War Crimes Tribunals.

80 For instance, the tribunal for the former Yugoslavia will never examine the responsibilities of General Bernard Janvier (head of the UN forces in the former Yugoslavia), Yasuhi Akashi (special envoy to the UN secretary general), and Commander Tom Karremans (head of the UNPROFOR battalion in Srebrenica) in the fall of Srebrenica and the massacre of 7,000 of its inhabitants. Similarly, the tribunal for Rwanda will not investigate the respective roles of French officers and diplomats — such as Lieutenant-Colonel Tauzin (a former military adviser of President Habyarimana who came back to Rwanda with operation Turquoise), the Lieutenants-Colonels Chollet and Maurin (the successive "commanders" and military advisers to the chief of staff of the Rwandan Armed Forces between 1992 and 1994), Ambassador Georges Martres, and Jean-Christophe Mitterrand and Bruno Delaye (the successive heads of François Mitterrand's African task force) — during the preparations for the Rwandan genocide.

81 For example, the Chilean Commission on Truth and Reconciliation was the first of its kind. It was created in 1990 by President Patricio Aylwin, the first elected president after sixteen years of military

dictatorship. In Argentina, to cite another case, a number of Argentinean officers, including the heads of the junta that ruled the country between 1976 and 1983, were tried and convicted for abductions, systematic torture, and murder, under the presidency of Raul Alfonsin—although they were later pardoned by President Carlos Menem.

82   Remarkably, just as the magistrates of the International War Crimes Tribunals managed to escape the so-called South American model of reconciliation, that same model received another blow, albeit a temporary one, with the arrest of Augusto Pinochet himself.

83   In the fall of 1999, however, the trial of Dinko Sakic, who ran the Jasenovac concentration camp until 1944, took place in Zagreb. Sakic, who had just been extradited by the Argentinean government at the request of the Croatian authorities, was convicted of war crimes—tens of thousands of Jews, Serbs, Gypsies, and antifascist Croats died in this most notorious camp of Pavelic's Croatia—and sentenced to twenty years in prison, the maximum punishment permitted for war crimes committed fifty years earlier.

84   Practically, such an identification is now close to being a reality since about two-thirds of the Serbs who lived in Croatia before 1991 left the country during the war. In particular, the 1995 reconquest of western Slavonia and the Krajina region provoked a massive exodus for which the Croatian army and Serbian militias of Milan Martic are equally responsible: the latter coerced their Serbian brethren into leaving before the arrival of the Croats—thereby creating the first wave of "self-ethnic cleansing"—while the former, despite Tudjman's promises, brutalized and intimidated most of the Serbs who had stayed. Needless to say, since the end of the war, the Croatian authorities have done nothing to facilitate the return of Slavonian and Krajina's Serbs.

85   On the eve of the war, about 44 percent of the Bosnians were Muslims—and as such, in the Yugoslav Federation, they were recognized as a nationality—31 percent were Serbs, and 17 percent were Croats. The remaining 8 percent usually called themselves Yugoslavs, either by political choice or because their origins were too mixed to claim any other nationality. In the 1990 elections, the three nationalist parties obtained about 70 percent of the vote: 30 percent for the SDA, 25 percent for the SDS, and 15 percent for the HDZ. Their postelectoral alliance was based on a common rejection both of the "ethnic-blind"

rhetoric professed by Tito's regime and the secular and largely intermixed culture of the cities. But beyond their shared commitment to a separatist brand of identity politics, the three parties favored decidedly different projects for the future of Bosnia. The SDA envisioned an independent Bosnia-Hercegovina where all citizens would have the same rights, but where the institutions and system of political representation would reflect the different demographic weights of the three communities. In other words, the Muslims would benefit from the privileges due a majority, albeit a relative one, while Serbs and Croats would be treated as well-protected and well-represented minorities. The SDS, on the other hand, wanted Bosnia to remain a Yugoslav republic where the Serbs would recover the status of "first among equals" that they had enjoyed under the Yugoslav monarchy of

King Alexander. As for the HDZ, its agenda was more complicated: its leaders supported Bosnia's independence in order to escape Serbian domination, but they also planned to gradually separate from Bosnia and rejoin Croatia. Therefore, despite their common determination to ward off the development of antinationalist forces, the three parties were clearly not meant to maintain their alliance for long.

86   A powerful member of the SDA, Abdic decided in 1993 that the Serbs had won the war. Since Izetbegovic could not be convinced to capitulate, he formed his own private army in the northwestern region of Bihac, made a deal with Mladic's militias, and turned his troops against the Bosnian army. Abdic's forces were defeated in 1994.

87   The story of Iran's intervention in the Bosnian War is emblematic of the strategy devised by the United States during the last year of the conflict. Once they had brokered the 1994 peace treaty between Croats and Muslims, U.S. officials decided that in order to pressure the Serbs into negotiating, it was time to arm their enemies. Both the UN arms embargo and official impartiality of the international community, however, prevented the United States from acting as a direct purveyor of military aid. The Clinton administration thus agreed to let the Iranian government provide equipment and even volunteers, through Croatia, to the Bosnian army. Now, considering the hostility between Washington and Tehran, why did the United States choose Iran — the rogue state par excellence — as its subcontractor? Though apparently absurd, such a choice was consistent with the objectives pursued

by the Clinton administration, which saw the Iranian intervention in Bosnia as the most efficient way of altering the balance of forces on the ground without modifying the official doctrine of the international community. In fact, both the Iranian implication in the conflict and subsequent "Islamization" of the main Bosnian institutions — since the influx of "Islamic" aid was bound to increase the influence of Muslim nationalists both in the government and army — provided the best possible justification for the continued impartiality of Western powers. For if it could be said that the Bosnian army and government were, respectively, infiltrated by Iranian-style "mujahedins" and dominated by local Islamic "fundamentalists," the credibility of Izetbegovic's regime as the protector of a multiethnic and democratic Bosnia would be gravely damaged. Hence, as the Clinton administration saw it, letting Iran arm the Bosnians served the double purpose of strengthening the Bosnia army in relation to their Serbian aggressors and weakening the image of the Bosnian regime in the eyes of the Western public. The combination of these two effects suited U.S. plans because it prepared the stage for a peace process where all the protagonists would be on a relatively equal footing, both materially and morally. (On Iran and the Bosnian War, see Roger Cohen, *Hearts Grown Brutal: Sagas of Sarajevo* [New York: Random House, 1998], 315–17, 408–9.)

88   While some of their detractors were sympathizers of the Habyarimana regime, and thus could hardly be considered trustworthy, others were longtime opponents of Hutu Power who initially welcomed the RPF victory. Among them, Faustin Twagiramungu and Seth Sendashonga were, respectively, prime minister and minister of the interior in the first RPF-led government of July 1994. Both of them resigned in protest during the summer of 1995 and subsequently went into exile, where their opposition to the Rwandan government increasingly hardened. In her book, *L'enjeu Congolais: L'Afrique centrale après Mobutu* ([Paris: Fayard, 1999], 235), Colette Braeckman reports that when he was assassinated in 1997 in Nairobi, Sendashonga was busy recruiting among Hutu refugees in Tanzania in order to enter the armed struggle against his former allies.

89   In October 1998, the Rwandan authorities started to deal with this huge problem by releasing 10,000 prisoners. They also attempted to

speed up the process by organizing collective trials and encouraging inmates to settle for plea bargains. Braeckman writes that this last measure became remarkably efficient after the government organized the public execution of twenty-eight convicts in January 1998 (*L'enjeu Congolais*, 223).

90 On the Kibeho massacre, see Philip Gourevitch, *We Wish to Inform You That Tomorrow We Will Be Killed with Our Families: Stories from Rwanda* (New York: Farrar Strauss and Giroux, 1998), 188–202.

91 Targeted by the Hutu militias based in UN refugee camps, many Banyarwandas from North Kivu and Banyamulenges from South Kivu — both of them Tutsis who had been living in Zaire for generations — were forced to flee to Rwanda between fall 1994 and winter 1996.

92 Even after its second offensive in the neighboring Congo — in the fall of 1998, this time against the Kabila regime — the RPA had still not succeeded in eliminating the threat of Hutu Power militias. Therefore, the Rwandan government decided to move the Tutsi settlers — about 400,000 people — away from the vicinities of Ruhengeri and Gisenyi. In other words, incapable of maintaining peace either by preaching reconciliation or by conducting systematic reprisals, the Rwandan authorities resorted to yet another policy imported from Burundi, namely, the systematic separation of Hutus and Tutsis.

93 President Mitterrand himself declared that one of the main tasks of operation Turquoise had been to prevent a "counter-genocide" against the Hutus. In November 1994, at the French-African summit of Biarritz, Mitterrand still referred to the events of the spring as "the civil war and the genocides that followed." Cited in Jean-Pierre Chrétien, *Le défi de l'ethnisme Rwanda et Burundi 1990–1996* (Paris: Karlhala 1997), 210–11.

94 Colette Braeckman has accurately emphasized the similarities between the position of the Rwandan authorities and that of the successive Israeli governments since 1948 (see *L'enjeu Congolais: L'Afrique centrale après Mobutu* [Paris: Fayard, 1999], 228–29). But there is also a strong resemblance between the type of racism faced by the Tutsis throughout central Africa and European anti-Semitism.

95 The political pressure exercised by the international community on the Serbian Republic took a plainly authoritarian turn in March 1999. Carlos Westendorp, the high representative for Bosnia-Hercegovina,

used the special powers he had received in 1997 from the committee in charge of implementing the Dayton Peace Accords to demote Nikola Poplasen, the ultranationalist president of the Republika Srpska. Moreover, a few days later, the representatives of the international community decided to make the city of Brcko a neutral district under international administration. (Conquered and brutally cleansed by Mladic's forces in 1992, Brcko was crucial to the Bosnian Serb authorities because it was the only passageway between the western and eastern parts of the Republika Srpska.)

96   An unsuccessful and increasingly isolated foe of Mobutu for about three decades, Kabila was nonetheless initially hailed as his country's liberator and a positive development for the entire African continent. Yet, once in power, he turned out to be a disappointment both for the Congolese people and his foreign sponsors. On the one hand, the populist and centralized regime that the self-proclaimed president of what is now the Democratic Republic of the Congo attempted to establish proved neither willing to meet the democratic expectations of the urban elites nor able to critically improve the living conditions of an extremely impoverished population. On the other hand, Kabila managed to alarm the representatives of the international community, both by curtailing the UN presence in the Congo and by choosing Chinese, Cuban, and Libyan business partners over Western companies. More important, he angered his protectors, Museveni and Kagame, who soon realized that Kabila was more anxious to escape their control than prevent the Hutu Power militias and Ugandan rebels known as the Lord's Resistance Army from using Congolese territory as their base. Caught between the discontent of his people and impatience of his sponsors, Kabila proved resourceful enough to pit his critics against one another. For while many Congolese were dismayed by the new regime, they were also increasingly outraged by the presence of Rwandan soldiers on their streets and Rwandan advisers in their country's government. Taking advantage of the resentment generated by the people who brought him to power, Kabila succeeded in defusing the mounting opposition to his rule by blaming the Congo's enduring problems on the nefarious influence of the Tutsis. Therefore, convinced that their former protégé had become uncontrollable and as dangerous as his predecessor, the Rwandan government and its Ugan-

dan ally decided to reproduce what they had done a year earlier—namely, mount another rebellion, once again with covert U.S. support, and install a new regime in Kinshasa.

97   Although the rebels, backed by Ugandan and Rwandan forces, initially seemed to be heading toward a rapid victory, Kabila succeeded in mustering enough support to retain control of Kinshasa and the western part of his country. In the Congo proper, the rebels were immediately, and accurately, perceived as pawns of the Rwandan army, which made them even less popular than Kabila. Moreover, the Congolese president managed to regain some clout by presenting his fight against the rebels as a "people's war" against the Tutsi invaders, and even by turning his anti-Tutsi propaganda into an open call for pogroms. The crucial support for Kabila did not come from his own people, however. The beleaguered Congolese dictator was rescued by other African leaders, primarily Eduardo Dos Santos of Angola and Robert Mugabe of Zimbabwe. Even though Dos Santos was hardly more satisfied than his Ugandan and Rwandan colleagues with Kabila's ability to protect his neighbors from rebels based on Congolese territory, he nonetheless decided to send troops into the Congo, both to save its besieged president and to destroy UNITA's bases. As for Mugabe, his motives for defending Kabila were at once personal—the two men had been friends since the 1960s—political—South Africa, Zimbabwe's regional rival, was perceived as siding with the rebels—and financial—Zimbabwean companies were deeply involved in the Congo's mining industry. The intervention of Angola and Zimbabwe, and to a much lesser extent Chad and Namibia—on Kabila's side turned the second Congolese war into a stalemate. The rebels eventually split into three different groups, while the relationship between their backers, Rwanda and Uganda, gradually deteriorated.

After a year of fighting, all the parties agreed to sign the so-called Lusaka Accord under the aegis of the Organization of African Unity but largely brokered by U.S. diplomats. According to the signed agreement: an international contingent mandated by the UN would disarm the various foreign rebels—the Rwandan and Burundan Hutu militias, Jonas Savimbi's UNITA, and the Ugandan rebels of the Lord's Resistance Army—operating on Congolese territory; a military commission involving all the warring parties would monitor the cease-fire; a government of national unity would be formed—including representatives of Kabila's party, the rebels, and the old political opposition to Mobutu—whose main task would be to organize a "national dialogue" leading to general elections; and foreign troops would leave the Democratic Republic of the Congo once the national dialogue was in place. Insofar as it both mandated the presence of Rwanda's protégés in the government of national unity and allowed for Rwandan troops in the Congo until Kigali considered the Hutu Power menace extinct, the Lusaka Accord was clearly serving Kagame's interests.

98 Regarding Africa, however, the new French president did not distinguish himself from his predecessors' inclination for old Francophone dictators. At the same time, following the Rwandan genocide, France no longer had the means to balance the U.S. influence in the region of the Great Lakes and, thus, challenge the new policies promoted by the State Department.

99 The lesson that U.S. officials had drawn from the three weeks of bombing prior to the Dayton accord was that creating a balance between the warring forces on the ground was a prerequisite for a "truly" even-handed diplomacy on the part of the international community. As we have seen, the 1998 report of the French parliamentary mission that set out to investigate France's role before and during the Rwandan genocide tried to use the same principle—help one side in order to level the field—to justify France's continued assistance to Habyarimana's regime.

100 During the summer of 1998, as the rebellion threatened to seize Kinshasa, thousands of Congolese Tutsis—as well as people thought to be Tutsis because of their physical appearance—were rounded up, arbitrarily detained, and in many cases, killed either by Kinshasa's police or "patriotic" mobs. The latter were encouraged by the Congolese state radio whose announcers used the same rhetoric as the Hutu Power propagandists of Radio Télévision Mille Collines in 1993 and 1994. Not surprisingly, Kabila's government not only appropriated the words of the Hutu Power militants but also joined forces with the remnants of the ex-FAR and Interahamwe militias still operating on Congolese territory.

101   Hence, the increasingly strained relations between Kagame and Museveni, whose designs for the northeastern portion of the Congo competed with those of his Rwandan counterpart.

102   In the spring of 1998, when the KLA's armed resistance prompted the Serbian government to trade systematic discrimination for brutal and massive repression, the leading members of the international community expressed their determination to avert a resurgence of violence in the Balkans. Yet despite their repeated claims that past mistakes would not be repeated, Western governments still dealt with Kosovo in a way that was reminiscent of their initial handling of the Bosnian War. As soon as the KLA clashed with the Serbian police, the situation in Kosovo was portrayed as the outbreak of yet another ethnic conflict fueled by two extremist parties. On the one hand, Western governments accused the Serbian authorities of using Albanian separatism as a pretext for maintaining Kosovo under military rule and depriving the Albanian majority of their civil rights. On the other hand, they accused the KLA militants of using Serbian authoritarianism as a pretext for challenging the internationally recognized borders of Yugoslavia. The international community, in other words, retrieved its traditional stance of a humanitarian and evenhanded mediator condemning violence on all sides and calling for a reasonable "middle ground" solution between two "extreme" positions. Even during the summer of 1998, the international community still reacted with little more than scolding and empty threats to the systematic destruction of Albanian villages by Serbian troops. Notwithstanding the alarming number of refugees — up to 250,000 at the beginning of the fall — and multiple reports of massacres, Western governments remained apparently faithful to their standard doctrine. Determined to persuade both Milosevic and the KLA that they would not support Kosovar separatism, they patiently waited for the Serbian army to demonstrate its military superiority over the Albanian guerrillas before seriously raising the threat of air strikes against Serbia.

103   In the United States, the most violent denunciations of Western policies in Bosnia and Rwanda were written by authors associated with what is usually called the liberal press by the Right and the mainstream press by the radical Left — namely the *New York Times, New*

Yorker, New York Review of Books, or even the right-of-liberal magazine, the *New Republic.*

104 Although usually more at ease than liberals with Western military expeditions, conservatives nonetheless insist that national security and the protection of Western investments abroad remain the guiding concerns of their countries' foreign policy. They thus argue that Western governments should not intervene in local and regional conflicts unless their own vital economic and political interests are at stake. Accordingly, most Western conservatives supported the Gulf War but saw no good reason for their troops to get involved in conflicts in Bosnia and Rwanda, where the outcome was not likely to affect Western interests in a crucial way. In all fairness, however, one should mention that a handful of notorious cold war "hawks" were among the few Western politicians who relentlessly advocated military action against Milosevic and his gang. Their rationale was simply that preventing the resurgence of genocidal practices on European soil — Africa never ranked so high on their agenda — was one of the responsibilities of Western democracies.

105 See, for instance, Noam Chomsky, *The New Military Humanism: Lessons from Kosovo* (Monroe, Maine: Common Courage Press, 1999).

106 Slavoj Žižek, "Against the Double Blackmail," *Nation,* 24 May 1999, 20.

107 Žižek, "Against the Double Blackmail," 22.

Michel Feher is a founding editor of Zone Books. He is the
author of *Conjurations de la Violence: Introduction à la
lecture de Georges Bataille*, and has edited *The Libertine
Reader: Eroticism and Enlightenment in Eighteenth-Century
France*, and with Ramona Naddaff and Nadia Tazi,
Fragments for a History of the Human Body (three volumes).

Library of Congress Cataloging-in-Publication Data
Feher, Michel.
Powerless by design : the age of the international
community / Michel Feher.
p.   cm. — (Public planet)
Includes bibliographical references.
ISBN 0-8223-2605-1 (cloth : alk. paper) —
ISBN 0-8223-2613-2 (pbk. : alk. paper)
1. Developing countries — Foreign relations.   2. World
politics — 1995–2005.   3. Security, International.
4. International relations.   5. Genocide.   6. Low-intensity
conflicts (Military science)   7. Ethnic relations.
I. Title.   II. Series.
D887 .F44   2000   327′.09′049 — dc21   00-039382